Eternal Life

and

A Course in Miracles

Eternal Life

and

A Course in Miracles

A PATH TO ETERNITY
IN THE ESSENTIAL TEXT

JON MUNDY, PhD

STERLING ETHOS
New York

STERLING ETHOS
New York

An Imprint of Sterling Publishing
1166 Avenue of the Americas
New York, NY 10036

ISBN 978-1-4549-1754-0

Distributed in Canada by Sterling Publishing Co., Inc.
c/o Canadian Manda Group, 664 Annette Street
Toronto, Ontario, Canada M6S 2C8
Distributed in the United Kingdom by GMC Distribution Services
Castle Place, 166 High Street, Lewes, East Sussex, England BN7 1XU
Distributed in Australia by Capricorn Link (Australia) Pty. Ltd.
P.O. Box 704, Windsor, NSW 2756, Australia

For information about custom editions, special sales, and premium and corporate
purchases, please contact Sterling Special Sales at 800-805-5489 or specialsales@
sterlingpublishing.com.

Manufactured in the United States of America

2 4 6 8 10 9 7 5 3 1

www.sterlingpublishing.com

You **will** undertake a journey
because you are not at home in this world.
And you "will" search for your home
whether you realize where it is or not.

If you believe it is outside you the search will be futile,
for you will be seeking it where it is not.

A COURSE IN MIRACLES T-12.IV.5:1–3

Heaven is your home,
and being in God it must also be in you.

A COURSE IN MIRACLES T-12.VI.7:7

Contents

Referencing *A Course in Miracles*

~~~~~~~~~~~~~~~~~~~~~~~~~

Quotations and paraphrasing from the Course, unless otherwise designated, come from the third edition, published by the Foundation for Inner Peace. The location of each quote or paraphrase appears immediately after the reference, followed by a listing of the chapter, section, paragraph, and sentence; for example, in T-9.III.4:1. "T" means "text"; "9" is the chapter; "III" is the section; "4" is the paragraph; and "1" is the sentence.

T is for *Textbook*
W is for *Workbook*
M is for *Manual for Teachers*
PI or PII *is for Part*
C is for *Clarification of Terms*
P is for *Psychotherapy: Purpose, Process, and Practice*
S is for *The Song of Prayer*
In is for *Introduction*
R is for *Review*
Ep is for Epilogue

A Course in Miracles is referred to throughout this text simply as "the Course." I sometimes put lines from the Course in **bold** for emphasis. Only rarely does the Course boldface a word or phrase within a sentence. However, some words that the Course has italicized for emphasis I have put in quotation marks to retain the emphasis, since the longer quotes from the Course are shown in italics. Bracketed words sometimes appear inside quotes from the Course so the reader will understand what the word "it" or "here" or "he," for example, refers to, as in "You will not see it [eternity] with the body's eyes" (T-20.II.8:3).

Most of the biblical quotations are from the King James Version, the version referenced within the Course and one of Dr. Helen Schucman's favorite translations.

If no source is given
for a centered alliteration,
epigram, poem, aphorism, or rhyme,
I have taken it from Heaven,
but I think it not a crime.
as it was a "given"
and it is no longer mine.

JON MUNDY

About *A Course in Miracles*

You were given everything when you were created,
just as everyone was.

T-1.IV.3:7

The 2008 Academy Award®–winning best picture of the year, *Slumdog Millionaire*, begins with the question "Is it written?" Is our destiny written in the Heavens? Do the individual choices we make lead us inevitably to the doors of eternity? According to the plot of the movie, circumstances in the life of slumdog Jamal Malik enable him to know the answer to every question on the Indian version of *Who Wants to Be a Millionaire?*—and not only does fate make him a millionaire; it leads him into the arms of Latika, his one true love. The last line in the movie is "It is written."

THE DIVINE PLAN—IT IS WRITTEN AND IT IS GIVEN

According to *A Course in Miracles*, not only is it written; it (the meaning of life) is also *given* to us; and our happiness depends upon our willingness to follow GPS—God's Plan for Salvation. The alternative is to follow the guidance of something we call an "ego," which leads us down an illusory path into a hellish state in which we feel separated from eternity. We can never lose God's Love. Hell can only come in *thinking* that we are separate from God. Hell is a thought and an illusion. Reawakening, renewal, and returning Home are always possible.

> *Whom God has called should hear no substitutes.*
> *Their call is but an echo of the original error that shattered*
> *Heaven.*
> *And what became of peace in those who heard?*
> *Return with me to Heaven,*
> *walking together with your brother out of this world*
> *and through another,*
> *to the loveliness and joy the other holds within it.*

T-18.I.12:1–4

IT IS GIVEN

The ancient Hindu and Buddhist sutras are regarded by Hindus and Buddhists as truth sayings that were *given* to a host of ancient teachers. In the Gospel of Matthew, Jesus says that it is not he who speaks but the Father who speaks through him, and he tells the disciples to take no thought for what they are to say, for the Father will speak through them (Matthew 10:19–20).

After meditating for many days in a cave, Muhammad said he was *given* the Koran, which he then recited to scribes. Three women saints within the Catholic tradition, Saint Hildegard of Bingen, Saint Bridget of Sweden, and Saint Teresa of Avila, all said their books were *given* to them. Saint Bridget of Sweden said that her whole book was given to her "in a flash."

The prolific Austrian composer Wolfgang Amadeus Mozart said he did not write his symphonies and concertos. They were *given* to him. Of course, Mozart knew how to write music. The famous Indian mathematician Srinivasa Ramanujan said he did not devise his mathematical theorems. He received his theorems, he said, through visions of scrolls of complex mathematical content unfolding before his eyes. He often said, "An equation for me has no meaning unless it represents a thought of God." Contemporary author and accomplished aviator Richard Bach said he did not write his book, *Jonathan Livingston Seagull*; it was given to him. As a talented aviator and stunt pilot, Richard Bach knew how to describe complicated aerobatic moves.

A Course in Miracles was *given* to Helen Schucman, PhD, a psychologist and professor at Columbia University College of Physicians and Surgeons in New York City. Helen had a deep, comprehensive understanding of psychology. She read her notes to her supervisor, Dr. William Thetford, and he typed up the books that became *A Course in Miracles*. Helen described what she heard as inner dictation. It began in October 1965 and ended in September 1972. *A Course in Miracles* was copyrighted in 1975 and published on June 22, 1976, by the Foundation for Inner Peace.

The Course consists of a *Textbook*, a *Workbook*, and a *Manual for Teachers*. After the Course was completed, there appeared two pamphlets from the same source as the Course: *Psychotherapy: Purpose, Process and Practice* (1975) and *The Song of Prayer* (1977). Total sales for the Course in all languages are in excess of 3 million copies; more than 2.5 million copies are in English, with the balance now in twenty-six different languages. Spanish is the second-bestselling edition, followed in order by German, Dutch, Portuguese, Italian, Swedish, and Chinese.

Public respect for the Course has grown consistently since its publication, and it is now regarded as a modern spiritual classic. The Course is incredibly deep, representing a level of psychological sophistication and understanding of the human psyche that simultaneously incorporates and transcends the wisdom of Sigmund Freud, Carl Jung, and other great psychologists and philosophers. It is reflective of the teachings of mystics of all faiths and all ages.

Though transcribed in the twentieth century, the Course is truly a twenty-first-century document. If the Course had appeared in, say, the nineteenth century, it simply would not have been understood.

I once ask Dr. Kenneth Wapnick, the leading spokesman for the Course, why he thought we received the Course during the latter quarter of the twentieth century. He said he did not know for sure but he was sure that we could not have received it until after Dr. Sigmund Freud appeared on the scene, as it was not until Freud that we had a clear ego psychology. Freud understood the ego very well. He explained to us how it works. Freud thought that we were damned with the ego, that it got worse as we got older, and that we died with it. Being an atheist, he did not see a way out. If he had studied the mystics, if he had studied Eastern philosophy, he might have realized that freedom from the ego and an awareness of eternity are quite possible.

This is a "required Course" (T-In.1:2). Another way to say this is, "Life is not an elective." Like it or not, we're here. Our main task is to live here happily, improving on our perspective, until such a time as we can see so far beyond this world that we begin to remember our true Home in Eternity. The Course says of itself that it is part of a "universal curriculum" (M-2.1:2). It is not an amalgamation of spiritual tradition. Rather, it represents a spiritual psychology that points to and then leads us Home. As Course teacher Ken Mallory says,

The Course came to us with the Love of God between the words.

Introduction

Perhaps *the* most glaring fact about this thing we call bodily life is that it ends. Indeed, as we age, we think all the more about mortality, knowing that bodily life on earth is headed progressively toward its end. I received a letter from an eighty-nine-year-old subscriber to *Miracles* magazine. In her letter she mused:

> Why am I still here, in a body which no longer works well? What purpose does this body serve? I am so filled with arthritis and pain. So many of my friends are now free of their bodies, but here I am, trapped in this wheelchair. I feel like I'm living in a prison. The pain in my spine is so dreadful. This body feels like a torture chamber. I hate having to have someone help me in the bathroom. I really don't enjoy being here.
>
> I try to be nice to the people who take care of me but my life is of service to no one and it's costing a fortune to keep me alive. Sometimes, I feel like Job from the Bible. Enough of forbearance! Why won't Jesus take me Home? I want to be done with this nursing home. Why not a funeral home? Why can't I go all the way Home?

FUNERALS

I prefer officiating at funerals to officiating at weddings and baptisms. Weddings and baptisms are joyful times, and yet we know 50 percent of all marriages will fail; thus what once was joyful becomes a time of sadness. I once saw a bride slap a groom prior to an expensive ceremony and knew for sure that marriage was doomed. It lasted only three months. Funerals are sad because a big hole is left in our lives. Funerals, however, also offer an opportunity for deeper connection. People's emotions are raw and open, and (assuming they are not sedated) they are more open to listening to and more capable of absorbing spiritual truths than they are on sleepy Sunday mornings.

Seeing a widow going through a service medicated on tranquilizers is always disheartening. Once back in the 1990s, I had a widow call me a few weeks after her husband's funeral. She asked me if I could tell her what I had said at her husband's service because she knew I had said something important but didn't know what it was. Being fully present to what one is feeling is the healthiest thing one can to do. Running away is never the answer. Grief should be faced straight on: tears should flow freely. Tears are sacred and crying is purification for the soul. A good session of crying will make anyone feel better. Facing death is a time of waking up, not a time of going to sleep. As Winston Churchill once said, "If you're going through hell, keep going."

A funeral service set up in the Protestant tradition includes a eulogy, the reading of scripture, some prayers, some music, and possibly memories of others who are willing to share. Then the minister has about half an hour to talk about life, death, and eternity, and no one is likely to stand up and propose a debate.

This book consists of three parts:

1. A description of my own encounters with death.

I have had three totally different experiences offering glimpses into eternity. The most profound was in 1976. I describe it in a section titled, "Holy Hell." "Holy Hell" were the last two words I said before I left this world. It was *holy* because of what came out of the experience, but *it was hell* on the ego level, as it meant an encounter with the end of this ego's *his-story*—its mythology.

Then there was a psychological encounter with death in 2001, when I was diagnosed with colon cancer. I had a tumor the size of a lemon removed from my insides, and on examination they found that the cancer had spread into my lymph system, so I had to face the real possibility that I might be facing death in the near future. Obviously, I survived.

The most peaceful experience, the third one, occurred in 2007 as the result of contracting La Crosse encephalitis virus from a mosquito bite, which placed me in a coma and out of commission for several weeks.

2. An examination of several mystical and near-death experiences. Of particular importance:

   A. Eben Alexander, MD's near-death experience as described in his book, *Proof of Heaven.*

   B. Anita Moorjani's extraordinary experience as described in *Dying to Be Me.*

3. An exploration of what this most incredible document called *A Course in Miracles* has to tell us about what these experiences mean and how it is we come to see into eternity.

FOLKS YOU'LL MEET IN THE COMING PAGES

Operas sometimes begin with an overture in which the characters in the opera are introduced before the story begins. In the same way, I would like to begin with a short introduction to the primary names you'll find repeated in the following pages.

My darling wife, Dolores, with whom I just keep falling in love, over and over again.

My oldest friend, Shanti Rica Josephs, who was with me at the time of my Holy Hell death encounter.

P.M.H. Atwater, an indefatigable researcher in near-death experiences, whom I met in 1978 when we were both giving talks on near-death experiences for the New Jersey Metaphysical Society. Atwater's most recent book, *Dying to Know You*, has been a valuable guide in my study of near-death experiences.

And my friend and companion on the road Home to God, Rod Chelberg, MD. Rod is the medical director for three nursing homes as well as Beacon Hospice in Bangor, Maine. He is an incredible loving man who has visionary experiences, sees auras, and prays with his patients. He is also an active student/teacher/facilitator of *A Course in Miracles*.

This book, like the Course itself, is about getting clearly centered on the path that leads to Heaven's door. Eventually, all mystical experiences include an awareness of eternity, which transcends what can be described in the limited framework of words. And yet we can use words to help us point the way. Socrates said he could not show us "the Good," but he might be able to show us what a child of the Good looked like. Then perhaps we would have some idea of what the Good was. As we cannot speak directly about what eternity is, we'll be saying a good deal about what it is not. Once we have freed ourselves from what is not true, what is true comes into view. Revelation will undo our own little made-up dreamworld and let us see another world our eyes could never find.

The course does not aim at teaching the meaning of love,
for that is beyond what can be taught.
It does aim, however, at removing the blocks to the awareness
of love's presence, which is your natural inheritance.

T-IN.1:6–7

SECTION 1

There's No Place Like Home

ONE

Impeccably on the Path

🌾

Ultimately, the goal of the Course
is understanding that you are not here.

DR. KENNETH WAPNICK (1942–2013)

By guiding your brothers home you are but following Him.

T-12.IV.5:7

As this book is about life, death, and eternity, I am compelled to begin with some reflections about Dr. Kenneth Wapnick—his life, his work, and his leaving of this world. This is the first book I've written since his passing on December 27, 2013, and I can't let his passing go without notice because his whole life was a lesson, a sermon, a teaching, and a story worthy of being told. He was a shining example of what it means to live a life dedicated to truth. His life was a demonstration that it is possible to accept the Atonement for oneself, showing us that "what he did, we too can do."

Ken was easily the kindest, wisest, most responsible, mature, and deeply loving man I'd ever met, and there are hundreds if not thousands who feel the same way. After Ken's passing, more than two hundred letters of commemoration were received at the Foundation for A Course in Miracles. He simply did what he was called to do.

He was focused, dedicated, and committed, and he lived his life in such a way that the *Holiness of the Creator shone through.* "To teach is to demonstrate" (M-In.2:1), and there was no one who better demonstrated the principles of the Course.

> *By accepting the Atonement for yourself,*
> *you are deciding against the belief that you can be alone,*
> *thus dispelling the idea of separation and affirming your true*
> *identification with the whole Kingdom as literally part of you.*
>
> **T-7.VIII.7:3**

SO SHALL YOU WALK THE WORLD WITH ME

In 1991, I wrote an article about Ken for *Miracles* magazine titled "Impeccably on the Path." I'd never met anyone as impeccable as Ken. Ken was not only my major teacher; he was and remains *the* major spokesman for *A Course in Miracles* for thousands. He was deeply committed to his work and he left us a mountain of information, in audio, video, and written form. In the space of thirty-five short years, he wrote some 32 books. He produced 208 CDs, 55 DVDs, and 206 YouTube presentations. Despite all this work, his main contribution was that he stood, and still stands, gently, patiently, and lovingly within the minds of all who studied with him as an example of the loving presence we can become. His very existence served as a beacon that said, "Come to the light that I have chosen."

MEETING HELEN AND BILL

The idea for my first book, *Learning to Die* (1973), came to me one morning as I was lying in bed thinking about all the funeral sermons I had written. It occurred to me that, properly arranged, there were enough of them to make a book. At the time, I was also working as the Executive Director of the Metropolitan New York branch of Spiritual Frontiers Fellowship. When I told one of the executives from the Spiritual Frontiers Fellowship national headquarters about my intentions of converting these sermons into a book, he asked that I send him a copy since they might like to publish the book—which they did.

Interestingly, it was through that book that I met Drs. Helen Schucman and Bill Thetford. One of the wonders of getting older is being able to look backward through the spectrum of life and see how one thing "had to" lead to another—how, as we have already noted, life is "given" to us—even *accidents*.

> *Remember that no one is where he is by accident,*
> *and chance plays no part in God's plan.*
>
> M-19.1:3

Learning to Die was published by Spiritual Frontiers Fellowship in 1973 and released at the organization's national conference in Chicago. I was there as a workshop leader. Author Hugh Lynn Cayce, son of American mystic Edgar Cayce, was the keynote speaker. Drs. Helen Schucman and William Thetford came to the conference, in part, to meet with Hugh Lynn. They also attended the lecture I gave on mysticism and near-death experiences.

I was one month short of my thirtieth birthday, and my experience and knowledge of mysticism paled in the face of Bill and Helen's experiences and knowledge. Fortunately, they were very kind and appreciative of my interest in mysticism. Helen, in particular, welcomed the fact that I was a young theologian. She did not, however, sit me down and tell me about the Course until April 20, 1975. That meeting took place in Ken's spartan little studio apartment on East Seventeenth Street in New York City.

At the end of that meeting, it was decided that Ken and I would get together for further talks. This we did in my office/apartment inside of General Theological Seminary, where I lived from 1971 to 1977 while doing graduate studies. I worked there as a part-time instructor while also teaching at the nearby New School university. Ken enjoyed coming to General Theological—modeled on an Oxford design with neo-Gothic buildings from the nineteenth century, facing a central quadrangle with tall sycamore trees. Chelsea Square is one of the secret architectural gems of New York City. From that first meeting on, I came to look upon Ken as a wonderful older brother, not only someone with whom I could share intellectually interesting ideas, but also someone I could go to in times of trouble and not be judged.

> *In each the other saw a perfect shelter*
> *where his Self could be reborn in safety and in peace.*
> *Such did his reason tell him;*
> *such he believed "because" it was the truth.*

T-22.I.9:8–9

Five weeks after my meeting with Ken, Helen, and Bill, they met Judy Whitson, head of the Foundation for ParaSensory Investigation in New York City. Judy realized immediately that the Course is what in philosophy is called "the philosopher's stone"—that which turns everything around and enables true vision. Judy and I had been friends since the 1960s. We were both active with the American Society for Psychical Research and were both teaching in the Continuing Education Department at New York University.

While Judy soon began to give talks on the Course and began the work of seeing that the Course got published, I started setting up lecture opportunities for Ken at my home, High Rock Spring, in Katonah, New York; at the church I was serving in Central Valley,

New York; and for Spiritual Frontiers Fellowship in New York City.

In 1979, I was commissioned by the Foundation for Religion and Mental Health to coordinate a series of Saturday seminars on psychotherapy and spirituality. I did one seminar with Ken and Father Benedict Groeschel and another with Dr. Thomas Hora on metapsychiatry and transpersonal psychology. Ken's future wife, Gloria, was sitting in the center aisle at the seminar. I remember seeing them "making eyes" and thought, *Something interesting is going on here.* They were married two years later.

Ken knew how to discipline without demanding. In the martial art of aikido, a master may, from time to time, slap a student to see how the student will react. Will the ego kick into gear and the student respond in anger? I asked Ken to be very honest with me in his comments on my writing. In this regard, Ken slapped me a few times—with the tongue, not the hand. If I was defensive, he would gently throw the ball back my way. Each time he did, I knew that he was right. With Ken and Helen, there was only their ever-steady presence. Ken set the bar high and pointed the way—with remarkable clarity. One of the things that amazed me was how he could be so loving, so strong, and so clear, and yet never did I feel attacked by him. Despite their "corrections," I never felt judged by Ken or Helen.

The "chosen ones" are merely those who choose right sooner.

T-3.IV.7:14

Despite his accomplishments, Ken was amazingly humble, rarely speaking of himself. On more than one occasion, he was asked to write his autobiography, and he always responded, "It's not about me."

The truly humble have no goal but God because they need no idols.

S-1.V.2

I once asked Ken about goals, and he said it is not about goals. Goals are usually of the ego. Our task in life is to find and follow the path set for us by God. Like Helen, Ken accepted his role in salvation and set about fulfilling the work he was called to do. He did it with class, cultivating along the way an amazing array of top-notch helpers—in addition to his wife, Gloria; Rosemarie LoSasso, PhD; Jeff Seibert, PhD; Loral Reeves; and his personal secretary, Elizabeth Schmit.

How is it that you sought me sorrowing?
Know you not that I must be about my Father's business?
(Jesus at age 12, speaking to his parents in the Temple.)
LUKE 2:49

You've heard of businesses starting in a garage. In 1981, I went to see Ken and Gloria when they were newly married and living in Gloria's home in Ardsley, New York, along with her aging parents. Gloria's mother really loved Ken. In a time before computers, Ken was working on the Glossary Index for A Course in Miracles. With Gloria's help, he had the entire Course indexed on three-by-five-inch cards in shoe boxes, sitting on card tables in the garage.

To fulfill the Will of God perfectly
is the only joy and peace that can be fully known,
because it is the only function that can be fully experienced.
T-8.III.2:1

Ken clearly knew that happiness lay in doing the greatest good he could, for as long as he could, for as many as he could. His happiness and his function were one. Like a Thomas Edison, a Nikola Tesla, or a Stephen Hawking, he poured himself into his work, loving every minute along the way.

In August 2013, I was in Southern California. Ken and I were going to have lunch on the fifteenth. The day before, I got a call from his secretary, Elizabeth, canceling the luncheon. In August 2011, he had canceled a luncheon date because he had to have emergency oral surgery. Though I never knew Ken to be sick, like all of us, he got older. Now he was canceling our luncheon date once again to go see the doctor.

Growing up in Brooklyn during the 1940s and '50s, Ken enjoyed playing stickball and baseball, so he wrote a funny note, which he asked Elizabeth to read over the phone. In the note he said that when he played baseball as a kid, he almost never struck out. He realized that canceling our luncheon was strike two. There would not be a strike three. The diagnosis, adenocarcinoma of the lung, stage four, meant that he would be around only long enough to say good-bye. Like my other mentor, Dr. Salvador Roquet, Ken knew a great deal about where he was going.

> *There is a light in you which cannot die;*
> *whose presence is so holy that the world*
> *is sanctified because of you.*
>
> W-156.4:1

Ken's light was very bright. He slept from ten p.m. to four a.m., just six hours per night. He was up early and working—inspired by the quiet morning air. He had a half day's work done while most of us were still sleeping. Ken's body died but his Spirit did not, because the Eternal cannot die. He got to go Home and, beyond the limited framework of the body and the body's eyes, see again his beloved Helen and his brother Bill. Speaking of the difference between the body and spirit, the Course says:

The frame is very elaborate, all set with jewels,
and deeply carved and polished.
Its purpose is to be of value "in itself,"
and to divert your attention from what it encloses.
But the frame without the picture you cannot have.

T-17.IV.7:5-7

It's not the frame (the body, the outside) that matters. It's the picture (spirit, the inside) that contains the heart's meaning. Thus, Principle 20 from the 50 Miracle Principles tells us that "miracles reawaken the awareness that the spirit, not the body, is the altar of truth." We let the world distract us into thinking that in and of itself, the body (the frame) is reality. Without spirit, the body is totally lifeless. It is my belief that Ken came so close to the Eternal—he moved so deep into Spirit—that he could no longer hold to the body, and thus, he blended back into Eternal Love. To remember God before one leaves the body is a beautiful way to go.

BRINGING THE MESSAGE HOME

Prior to Helen's leaving this world, Ken's life was dedicated to her and to the work they shared. He was clearly the son she never had, as Judy Whitson was her daughter. More than anyone, he brought to us the profound message of this incredible document we call "the Course."

If you would but let the Holy Spirit tell you of the Love of
God for you,
and the need your creations have to be with you forever,
you would experience the attraction of the eternal.
No one can hear Him speak of this
and long remain willing to linger here.

> *For it is your will to be in Heaven,*
> *where you are complete and quiet,*
> *in such sure and loving relationships that any limit is impossible.*
> *Would you not exchange your little relationships for this?*
> *For the body "is" little and limited,*
> *and only those whom you would see without the limits the ego*
> *would impose on them can offer you the gift of freedom.*

T-15.IX.5:1–5

THE ATTRACTION OF THE ETERNAL

There was once a GEICO auto insurance commercial in which the company's mascot, a gecko with an English accent, got a little too close to a vacuum tube, and *swish*, up and away he went. I think Ken got a little too close to "the attraction of the Eternal," and he slipped on over. He accomplished in one short life what a dozen other men might have done, all the while never losing sight of his Father and his Heavenly Home.

> *Remember always that you cannot be anywhere*
> *except in the Mind of God.*

T-9.VIII.5:3

One of the things that happens as we study the Course is the subtle realization that "someone greater than I" is running the show. As Jesus says in the Gospels, "It is not I that live but the Father that lives within me." This is experienced as growing *awareness* and the acceptance of *responsibility*. Ken was amazingly aware and responsible, so much so that . . . this is what I think happened to Ken; his wife, Gloria, agrees:

Sometimes a teacher of God
may have a brief experience of direct union with God.
In this world, it is almost impossible that this endure.
It can, perhaps, be won after much
devotion and dedication,
and then be maintained for much of the time on earth.
But this is so rare that it cannot be considered a realistic goal.
If it happens, so be it. If it does not happen, so be it as well.
All worldly states must be illusory.
[This next sentence may explain it all:]
If God were reached directly in sustained awareness,
the body would not be long maintained.

M-26.3.1–8

If there was ever anyone who was devoted and dedicated, it was Ken. How appropriate that our first Course teacher should have demonstrated that the Atonement can indeed be completed. He had to complete it so we could see the way ourselves. I remember Ken saying that "once we have completed the Atonement, there will then be no need to make up a world of bodies and, thus, a world in which there is war, disaster, and disease." It is our job through true vision to see beyond the hell of this world into Eternity. Only in this way is hell turned into Heaven—Heaven by definition being a state of perfection.

In the Gospel of John (16:7), Jesus, speaking of his impending bodily death, says, "It is to your advantage that I am going because unless I go, the Comforter [the Holy Spirit] cannot come to you." The disciples were, no doubt, so enamored of Jesus that they did not realize that the same Spirit that spoke to and through him could also speak to and through them. Now that Ken's body is gone, those of us who relied so much on him must rely evermore on this same "Christ within." As Judy Whitson said, "Ken's dying proves you can be in this world but not of it."

Minds need not the body to communicate.

T-20.V.5:3

I was once asked at a workshop if we were not obliged to keep reincarnating until such a time when everyone was enlightened. Let's remember that, as it says in the quotation earlier in this section, "all worldly states must be illusory," and enlightenment "is so rare it cannot be considered a realistic goal." Why should we think that we need to return again into bodily form to be helpful? Who says spirit cannot be present in this world? Does one help a child to grow by becoming once again a child? The body is an illusion. Someday it will disappear. The whole of the "outside" world is an illusion. Someday it will disappear. That which is Eternal lasts forever and cannot disappear.

For grandeur is the right of God's Son,
and no illusions can satisfy him or save him from what he is.
Only his love is real, and he will be content only with his reality.

T-13.III.8:6–7

THE PASSING OF BILL AND HELEN

It seems appropriate to speak about the passing of Dr. Helen Schucman (February 8, 1981) and Dr. William Thetford (July 4, 1988) as well, as they along with Ken were the major players in the production and principal teachings of the Course.

The first major teachers of the Course—Bill, Ken, and, in the end, the most resistant, Helen—came, I believe, to a complete acceptance of the Atonement. Though Helen understood the Course very well and she could teach it, she had a love/hate relationship with the Course. When she complained that the Course was not working for her, Jesus gently admonished her, saying, "Why don't you do what I'm asking you to do, so you can hear my voice even better?" That line is for us all.

Helen's Last Day

Ken and Helen's husband, Louis, were with Helen in the hospital on February 8, 1981. As her condition appeared to be stable, the night nurse suggested that Ken and Louis go home. Then shortly after eleven p.m., the hospital staff called to say that she had died. Folks often leave when nobody is there—no one except for God. My mother, Milly, died at home on Christmas Day 2001. I was sitting next to her bed, holding her hand and thinking of the many wonderful Christmas days she had created for our family. I kept saying, "Momma, it's Jon; I'm here. Momma, it's Jon; I'm here." My sister, Ann, came to the bedroom door and asked if I would come to the kitchen for a moment to speak with her. In those brief five minutes while we were in the kitchen, Mother passed. It's as though folks need to be alone when they leave this world—because they are not alone. Christ always comes—be his name Allah or Jehovah, Jesus, or Buddha. God does not understand our speech—only the words of our hearts.

Jesus told Helen that he would come for her, and Ken said that when he returned to the hospital, Helen's face had a remarkably quiet expression of peace that spoke convincingly of an experience of knowing. Her beloved Jesus had kept his promise, and she had kept hers (see Dr. Kenneth Wapnick, *Absence from Felicity*, page 472).

> *For what is Heaven but union, direct and perfect,*
> *and without the veil of fear upon it?*
> *Here are we one, looking with perfect gentleness*
> *upon each other and on ourselves.*

Here all thoughts of any separation between us
become impossible.
You who were a prisoner in separation
are now made free in Paradise.
And here would I unite with you,
my friend, my brother and my Self.

T-20.III.10:3–7

BILL'S LAST DAY

Bill came to Judy Whitson's home in Tiburon, California, to celebrate the Fourth of July in 1988 with a group of friends. Judy said there was a radiance about him. He started dancing around her living room. "Bill," Judy said, was "tripping the light fantastic." "I feel so flexible; I'm feeling so free!" he exclaimed. "All my relationships feel so completely healed and whole!" That evening at dinner, Bill told his friend Catherine, "There's no baggage. I'm cleaned out—in and out. I'm complete with everyone." The next morning, on his way out for a walk, the surgeon who lived next door to Judy saw Bill collapse, and he said, "Bill's heart just blew out."

Whenever you are in doubt what you should do,
think of His Presence in you,
and tell yourself this, and only this:
He leadeth me and knows the way, which I know not.
Yet He will never keep from me what He would have me learn.
And so I trust Him to communicate to me
all that He knows for me.

T-14.III.19:1–4

I Want To Go Home

———————————————————

This world you seem to live in is not home to you.
And somewhere in your mind you know that this is true.
A memory of home keeps haunting you,
as if there were a place that called you to return,
although you do not recognize the voice,
nor what it is the voice reminds you of.

W-182:1:1–3

When birds are migrating to other lands, the instinct to migrate is strong. If a migratory bird is put into a cage, it will pace back and forth. It will beat its breast against the bars. It will do everything in its power to get out of the cage. If the same bird is put into a cage when it is not migration time, however, the bird will not try to break free. Throw it up into the air, and it won't fly too far away. The tug at the heart is gone.

Something tugs at the heart. We want to be at Home with God. We want to fully be the Love we are. Every soul strives to rise above the mundane. Everyone hungers for Heaven, for rest, and for Eternal Peace beyond our often stressful, restless, and unsatisfying lives. We need a refuge from the rat race and the struggle for survival. We long for a life that fulfills our deepest yearnings, past all the nonsense of the world—into a life of meaning.

Your home has called to you since time began,
nor have you ever failed entirely to hear.
You heard, but knew not how to look, nor where.
And now you know. In you the knowledge lies, ready
to be unveiled and freed from all the terror that kept it hidden.

T-20.II.8:5–8

I especially enjoyed the pastoral aspects of ministry. Taking care of the older folks was particularly fun. Everybody loves to be loved, and the more attention I gave them, the happier they were. I realized that for some of the older women, that five-second hug in the church vestibule on Sunday morning was the only overt display of affection they received from a man. I can still remember Mildred Clark. Barely five feet tall, she would virtually quake as she stood in line with half a dozen other older women waiting for the Sunday morning peck on the cheek.

One of the members of the church was an older woman named Mrs. Voight, who was a shut-in. As she could not come to church, I would make monthly calls to her home to give her communion and spend time visiting with her. Mrs. Voight was fairly wealthy and could afford a full-time live-in housekeeper/nurse. On six or more occasions, the nurse called me saying she thought Mrs. Voight was dying. I would go, but Mrs. Voight would not die.

Finally, the day came when the nurse called and said she thought Mrs. Voight really was dying and I should come. I went and, indeed, Mrs. Voight was dying. As the nurse and I stood by her bed, Mrs. Voight began to cry, saying, "I want to go Home! I want to go Home!" I don't think what followed would happen in the twenty-first century, since the training of nurses is now more sophisticated when it comes to handling the dying. But this occurred in the early 1970s, and as Mrs. Voight was hard of hearing, the nurse, who was standing next to me, said rather loudly, "Now, nonsense, Mrs. Voight! You are home!" Meaning, she was in her apartment in Brooklyn.

Mrs. Voight was weary of her body, which was old and sick and tired, and she wanted to go Home. Although I might not have done this with a close family member, I turned to the nurse and asked her if she would leave us alone for a few minutes, as I wanted to say some prayers in private for Mrs. Voight.

Mrs. Voight and her nurse clearly had what the Course calls a "special relationship" (based on control and expectations, rather than love and forgiveness). The moment the nurse left the room, Mrs. Voight opened her eyes, which had been closed up to that moment. She did not say anything. She just lay there staring at me with an expression on her face that seemed to be saying, "Help me!" I said, "Mrs. Voight, you can go Home whenever you want to." A tear began to run down her cheek; she smiled a little smile and said, "Thank you." She closed her eyes, and before too long, I invited the nurse to come back into the room. Mrs. Voight had gone Home. Her real Home was not a body in an apartment in Brooklyn.

When I told this story in a workshop in Syracuse, New York, Cybie Mauro (an old friend and workshop participant) told a nearly identical story about being with her mother at the time of her death. She and her sisters were all in her mother's bedroom in her mother's house when Cybie's mother also started saying, "I want to go Home!" And when, just like Mrs. Voight's nurse, one of Cybie's sisters pointed out to her mother that she was in her home, her mother exclaimed, "No, not this home!"

Where does Dorothy want to go in *The Wizard of Oz*? Home. Where does Alice want to go in *Alice in Wonderland*? Home. Where does the boy in the modern fairy tale *The Polar Express* want to go? Home.

Where is Dorothy? Dorothy has bumped her head, and she is suffering from a concussion. She is in her bed on her aunt Em's farm in

Kansas, surrounded by those she loves. All the while, she is dreaming she is in a strange land called Oz.

Where is Alice? She is sound asleep with her head on her sister's lap, lying under a stately tree, dreaming she is in a topsy-turvy world somewhere down a rabbit hole.

Where is the boy in *The Polar Express*? He is on a wild train ride to the North Pole, and yet he is tucked away safely in his bed. When he awakens, it will be Christmas morning.

One of the students in our Miracles in Manhattan class, Cora Yumul, had a near-death experience. She was supposed to have a hysterectomy, but the doctor could not proceed with the operation, as Cora started bleeding badly. Cora was wearing a "Do Not Resuscitate" bracelet, and she died for ninety-nine seconds, during which time she watched "from above" as the operating room staff, in a panicked state, tried to figure out if they should attempt to save her life. Obviously, they brought her back. When she told our Miracles class about her experience, she waved her hand in front of her face as if to cool herself and said, "Whew, I didn't want to come back; over there—that *is* Home."

The Journey Home

In *The Pilgrim's Progress* (published in 1678), John Bunyan tells about the wonders of the mystic's journey. After the parables of Jesus, *The Pilgrim's Progress* is the most famous Christian allegory. Bunyan wrote his epic work while in prison for "preaching without a license." Translated into more than two hundred languages, it was required reading in Protestant schools throughout the eighteenth and nineteenth centuries. It was the next bestselling book after the Bible until the twentieth century.

It is the story of a hero named Christian who goes off in search of the Celestial City (Heaven). He is carrying on his back a number of burdens, and he must go through a series of experiences: "The Slough of Despond," "The Valley of Humiliation," and even "The Valley of the Shadow of Death." As he goes through these various experiences, his burdens are lifted from him until he arrives at the Celestial City completely naked (unburdened).

> *Jesus said, "The world is a place of transition, full of examples:*
> *be pilgrims therein, and take warning by the traces*
> *of those that have gone before."*
> **NEAL ROBINSON**, *CHRIST IN ISLAM*

From the most primitive mythological traditions to sophisticated twenty-first-century societies, there are stories of heroes and heroines who go off in search of a greater destiny than sleeping, eating, earning a living, raising a family, and dying. The hero leaves home and ventures into a strange land, encounters difficulties, and falls prey to a variety of forces and illusions. Here, too, the hero meets a guide who provides tools to help in a journey that involves some task, some mission, some specific function.

THE INNER GUIDE

Helen Schucman once said that the purpose of the Course was to help us get in touch with our Inner Teacher. Course students are called upon to develop an "inner dialogue" with Spirit. Bernadette Roberts (author of *The Experience of No-Self: A Contemplative Journey*) calls it a "Unitive Life." The mystic tunes in to what Native Americans call "The Great Man in the Heart" or what fellow Course friend and teacher Mary Gerard Lenihan calls "the Mentor Within." With practice, we can begin to differentiate between the anxious voice of the ego and the "still, small Voice" for God. The question is not, "Is there an inner voice?" The question is, "Why don't I do what he asks me to do, so that I can hear his Voice even better?"

There is not in the world a life more sweet and delightful, than that of a continual conversation with God. Only those who comprehend it can practice and experience it.

FRENCH MYSTIC BROTHER LAWRENCE (1614–1691)

Words can be helpful, particularly for the beginner, in helping concentration and facilitating the exclusion, or at least the control, of extraneous thoughts.

M-21.1:8

THE WORD

The inner guide often provides a tool to help our hero throughout the spiritual journey. In Catholicism, these various tools are sometimes called "attributes." The tool might be knowledge, motivation, patience, psychic ability, or some kind of useful object: a paintbrush, a guitar, or in today's world, a computer. The "Word" is the most common of all tools and guides. It is often in the form of a book: the Bible, the Upanishads, or other scripture. Moses is given the Ten Commandments, Mohammed receives the Koran, and we now have *A Course in Miracles*.

In relating my 1976 near-death experience, I describe a web, or grid, that delineates a new but very familiar universe. In fact this universe was the most familiar thing there is. It was where we all are, where we always have been. In her book, *Dying to Be Me*, which described her near-death experience, Anita Moorjani spoke with her father in the afterlife and said:

> Dad, it feels like I've come home! I'm so glad to be here.
> Life is so painful! I told him.
> But you're always Home, darling, he impressed upon me.
> You always were, and you always will be. I want you to remember that.

Heaven waits for his [your] return,
for it was created as the dwelling place of God's Son.
You are not at home anywhere else,
or in any other condition.
Do not deny yourself the joy that was created for you
for the misery you have made for yourself.
God has given you the means for undoing what you have made.
Listen, and you will learn how to remember what you are.

T-10.V.11:3–7

We are all waiting to be called Home, and the good news is, as we'll see in the coming pages, we don't have to die in order to go Home.

THREE

Mystical and
Near-Death Experiences

*Everyone has experienced what he would call
a sense of being transported beyond himself. . . .
It is a sense of actual escape from limitations.
If you will consider what this "transportation" really entails,
you will realize that it is a sudden unawareness of the body,
and a joining of yourself and something else
in which your mind enlarges to encompass it.*

T-18.VI.11:1, 3,4

As long as we have thought, we've longed to know what's really going on. What is the meaning behind this thing we call "Life," or does it even have a meaning? Is what we call "life" limited to one brief experience of a biological organism, which lasts perhaps eighty years, and then that's it? Voilà! The lights go out forever? Are we in agreement with British philosopher, Bertrand Russell, who said, "I believe that when I die, I shall rot"?

As long as we have been able to speak, there have been those who have told us of unusual experiences in which they have been able to see beyond the obvious, to connect with higher wisdom, or to see things not accessible to the body's eyes, ears, and other senses.

Your chosen home is on the other side,
beyond the veil.
It has been carefully prepared for you,
and it is ready to receive you now.
You will not see it with the body's eyes.
Yet all you need you have.

T-20.II.8:1–5

A HOLY INSTANT

What is being depicted in the passage above is often called a mystical experience. Mystical experiences are frequently described in the Course as "a Holy Instant"—a moment in which we are temporarily able to see through the eyes of Spirit (or the mind of Christ) instead of an ego. A Holy Instant is a little opening—a memory of Eternity.

In these instants of release from physical restrictions,
you experience much of what happens in the holy instant;
the lifting of the barriers of time and space,
the sudden experience of peace and joy, and,
above all, the lack of awareness of the body,
and of the questioning whether or not all this is possible.

T-18.VI.13:6

Ken's early mystical stirrings came to him while lying on the floor in his parents' apartment in Brooklyn listening to classical music. As I grew up on a farm in Missouri during the 1940s and '50s, nature provided a portal that enabled my taking a peek into the Eternal. The following is a description of a mystical experience, a Holy Instant, by Rod Chelberg, MD:

My experience was that my entering the Holy Instant flips a switch that completely turns off time and space for EVERYTHING. Time and space simply stop . . . a dead stop. Time and space cease to exist for everything. When I exited time and space, the cosmos "turned off." It seems that either we are all in the "world" or it shuts down. I have no reason to believe that this phenomenon is different for anything other than myself. Since I am no different from anything else, whenever any of us experience a Holy Instant (become present) the cosmos simply ceases to exist for everything until the sojourner returns from the present to the past. Then the illusion continues from where it left off when the sojourner existed in the physical. This is why only one "Teacher of God" is needed to save (awaken) the world. [M-12] When any one of us makes the Holy Instant his/her only instant, everything is healed and everything awakens from the dream of death. Presto . . . it's over!

A mystical experience that almost everyone can identify with is falling in love, where *something seems to take over* inside, something much bigger than the selfish little self that often dominates our thinking. Something wholly new takes hold of us and we want to shout it from the rooftops. We *fall in love*; we tumble into the experience as though we were free-falling through space, because we are free and we are falling—only it's into the arms of God. Of course, all the while we fall, the ego keeps peeking its head out—on guard, looking out for some obstruction that might be used to upset our bliss. Falling in love is heavenly. Losing a love is hell. When we are in love, our biggest joy is in sharing with the beloved. Then indeed we know that giving and receiving are one in truth.

> *Projection makes perception.*
> *The world you see is what you gave it,*

nothing more than that.
But though it is no more than that, it is not less.
Therefore, to you it is important.
It is the witness to your state of mind,
the outside picture of an inward condition.

T-21.IN.1:1–5

The basic difference between a mystic and what I call a *regular* person is that *a regular person*—that's most all of us, most all of the time—*is a projector.* We are making up the world and we don't know that we're doing it. Indeed, we claim to be at the mercy of the world. However, *a mystic is a receptor.* A mystic simply sees without evaluation, judgment, comment, or condemnation. The ego is addicted to finding problems, pointing them out, and talking about them—always whatever is wrong in the world is seen on the outside. It is not inside of me.

The mystical state is actually the "normal" state. Being projectors means we see only what we project. Being able to see without projection is a mystical state. It is also a miraculous state. Miracles are nature. Love is natural, vision is natural, communion is natural, peace is natural, joy is natural, and Heaven is our native Home. Since our real Home is Heaven and our *natural* way of thinking is in line with the Mind of God, seeing ourselves as separated and sinful or capable of *thinking outside of the Mind of God is unnatural* and requires a false adjustment in the mind (T-12.VII.4).

As it is, we've got what is natural and unnatural twisted around and backward. We've been looking for the inside on the outside, where it cannot be found. We need a reversal in thinking. That is, rather than continuing to project, blame, judge, analyze, interpret, and condemn, we need to stop all such insanity and engage in a reversal in thinking. It seems as if the world determines what we perceive. A reversal in thinking enables true vision. *Our thoughts determine the world we see.*

Our "normal" "adjusted" state is too often the abdication of
ecstasy, the betrayal of our true potentialities.

R.D. LAING (1927–1989), SCOTTISH PSYCHIATRIST

The journey through the illusions of this world is not an easy one. We find ourselves in situations where we are unable to conform to the conflicting and often contradictory expectations from parents, society, and the culture of which they are a part. According to Scottish psychiatrist, R.D. Laing, the church, with all of its many ambiguous constructs, mythologies, dogmas, creeds, and doctrines, has made it difficult for us to live natural lives.

Take, for example, the situation in which folks experience post-traumatic stress disorders. Soldiers are put into situations where their bodily lives are in danger, and then they are asked to kill other people (a most unnatural act) as though it were the right thing to do. War is unnatural. It is division, not increase. There is no war in Eternity—how could there be? If there were, it would not be Heaven. In the words of Civil War General William Tecumseh Sherman, "War is hell!" Hell is a state of war. Heaven (our natural state) is by definition a place of joy and Eternal peace.

NEAR-DEATH EXPERIENCES

There has been a growing number of descriptions of near-death experiences in the past few years, not because more people are having these experiences; rather, more people than ever are now able to place their fingers on computer keys and write up a description of what they have seen and have it published online, in an e-book, or in a regular book format. Never before have we had such an opportunity to study in such depth the nature of life after life. In some cases, as with Dr. Eben Alexander's *Proof of Heaven*, the book made it to the *New York Times* bestseller list. While it is not necessary to have a near-death experience to have a mystical experience, all near-death experiences are inevitably otherworldly and, therefore, mystical.

PRIMARY CHARACTERISTICS OF MYSTICAL EXPERIENCES

There is an ineffability quality: The experience cannot adequately be described in words. Sometimes a whole new way of communication is achieved. A new language appears—not English or anything man-made, yet somehow intuitively knowable.

1. The experience is timeless and spaceless. In other words, the experience defies form.

William Blake expressed it best when he said that from the mystical perspective we can

See a World in a Grain of Sand
And Heaven in a Wild Flower
Hold Infinity in the palm of your hand
And Eternity in an hour.

WILLIAM BLAKE, ENGLISH MYSTIC, POET, AND PAINTER (1757–1827)

2. There is a deep noetic (knowing) quality, including the sense that one knows everything there is to be known, together with an awareness of immortality and freedom from a fear of death. Or it may just be pure knowing, what the Course calls Perfect Knowledge (T-5.II.5:1).
3. There is a sense of sacredness, blessing, and beneficence and the feeling that one is in the presence of the Divine.
4. There is a profound sense of union or connectedness with all

living things, indeed in this world and beyond, even with the rocks, trees, and stars.

5. There is often (though not necessarily) a visionary quality. Mysticism can simply be an "awareness" without form.

6. There is a deep sense of peace. The experience is happening to and through you. You cannot direct or manipulate the experience, and if you try to direct it, you will lose the experience.

7. Mysticism is just a way of seeing. It is an *in-sight* you know is true. With eyes closed, the individual may experience incredibly vivid pictures, detailed patterns, designs, and structures. With eyes open, the individual may see plants seeming to breathe. Light may be seen around objects.

When we dream at night, where are the eyes that do the seeing? Complicated, intricate patterns and objects can be seen; people talk to us; buildings, trains, cars, rivers, and mountains may appear in our dreams. But where are these "things"? Certainly, it's not the body's eyes that are doing the seeing. In the same way, in visionary experiences, it is the mind's energy that gives us sight.

Access to Mystical States

Let's examine the various ways in which folks come to some sort of mystical awakening.

1. *A Course in Miracles* began after William Thetford, PhD, head of the Department of Psychology at Columbia University College of Physicians and Surgeons, tired of the bickering, backbiting, and one-upmanship that characterized his own department, turned to his assistant, Dr. Helen Schucman,

and said, "There has to be another way," meaning there had to be some way they could get along with each other without all of the ego games going on within their own department. Uncharacteristically, Helen turned to Bill and said, "You're right. I'll help you find it." That was in some sense the first miracle of the Course. Two psychologists at a prestigious university who had been antagonistic toward each other agreed in love to find, once and for all, a way out of their own insanity. Miraculously, they found that way.

Crash and Burn—Despair and Depression

The Alister Hardy Religious Experience Research Centre at the University of Wales has collected, online, more than six thousand descriptions of mystical experiences. According to the center's research, the number one stimulant for a mystical experience is despair and depression, sometimes accompanied by a profound crash-and-burn experience, which signals a giving up on the ways of the world and a deepening need for a way of seeing outside of the insanity of the ego. In classic mystical literature, this state was described as the Dark Night of the Soul by Spanish mystic, Saint John of the Cross (1542–1591). According to the Course, depression is the sign of allegiance to the god of sickness.

Depression means that you have forsworn God.

T-10.V.1:3

Of course, it's not the depression that brings us Home; it's hitting bottom and then experiencing an inevitable revelation—a turnaround and the experience of freedom, perhaps even in the face of death. If we give up completely on the ways of the world; if we crash and burn finally, fully, and utterly; if we throw all our ego baggage away, then we have an opportunity for seeing, free of blinders. There may be a literal crash. Many near-death experiences occur in automobile and industrial accidents and on battlefields. When it looks as though this life is over completely, a whole new way of seeing often becomes possible.

> *If you know you're going to be hung in the morning,*
> *it helps to concentrate the mind.*
> SAMUEL JOHNSON, 1709–1784

Here, Too, Is Heaven

I think the first thing that happens to us when we die is that we say to ourselves, *Well, I'm still here*, meaning, awareness has not been lost. The body disappears, but Spirit, not being made of matter, cannot expire. Such was the case for my friend, Veronica Viddler, who had a profound mystical experience when she had a massive heart attack while lying on a gurney in a hospital. Thinking she was going to die, rather than being fearful, she accepted her fate and then entered into a place of deep peace where she knew that whatever happened, God's Will would prevail and she would be okay.

2. Mystical experiences often occur as a result of an illness, especially an illness with high fever; during a crisis in personal relationships, such as a divorce; when grieving over the loss of a loved one, especially in the face of an unexpected loss such as the death of a child or a spouse; during a bankruptcy; or during an attempted suicide or when we think we are going to die. What happens when we give in completely is

that we realize, *I'm still here.* The mind is still thinking. The mind keeps on because it is Eternal. On the more positive side, mystical experiences may occur during painfully blissful moments, like the birth of a child.

3. One of the most fun ways the mystical comes to us is in the loss of oneself while engaged in creative works. Art, dancing, sculpting, building, decorating, gardening, and writing, of course, are all wonderful alchemical ways to find Eternity's door. What joy to lose oneself in a painting, a poem, or any project that brings a sense of accomplishment. What bliss it is to feel the creative juices flowing freely.

4. Most mystical experiences occur when we are alone. Mystical experiences may occur while meditating or just becoming deeply relaxed. They can happen when we are with other people while chanting, perhaps, but it's more likely that there will be no external stimuli demanding our attention.

5. Mystical experiences may occur while taking psychedelics or anesthetic drugs. Many near-death experiences occur during surgery.

6. One of the most common stimulants to a mystical experience is being in nature. This was true for me as a farm boy in Missouri in the 1950s. At the age of fourteen, I was hunting alone in the woods on the back of our farm, and, while "freezing" (standing perfectly still), for some unknown reason I stopped thinking and experienced a kind of pure seeing without the contamination of thought. What brought me back was the thought, *What is having this experience?* And I heard a voice that said, "Who wants to know?" That's all it said, but that was enough. Here is a nature mysticism description from American Transcendentalist, Ralph Waldo Emerson, in his book, *Nature*:

*Standing on the bare ground, my head bathed in the blithe air
and uplifted into infinite space, all mean egotism vanishes.
I become a transparent eyeball. I am nothing. I see all.
The currents of universal being circulate through me.
I am part and parcel of God.*

How did Emerson come to this experience? By being nothing. Only then was he able to see all. By giving up everything, by letting the story go completely—then and only then is it possible to see all.

7. Mystical experiences may occur for no apparent reason. You may be alone, perhaps in your bedroom, or maybe just sitting in your car or house, and suddenly you are "not there." The experience may come early in the morning before the mind is filled with thoughts about the day. A sense of complete serenity and peace may come over you while you are driving home from work, just sitting alone in your room, walking, reading, cooking, or bathing—anything at all.

    P.M.H. Atwater describes what she calls "near-death-like-experiences." She describes, for example, how on a Sunday morning, a woman was bending over to pick up the Sunday morning newspaper on her porch, and after straightening up, she looked into the rising sun and somehow seemed to enter it. There she had a full-blown near-death experience similar to those reported in automobile accidents or on operating tables (Atwater, *Dying to Know You*, page 58).

Two students told me of a similar mystical experience that occurred while they were sitting cross-legged on a bed, relaxing after a busy day of work.

Here is a description of a mystical experience told by Bonnie McKim, from Corydon, Indiana. Bonnie attended a week-long workshop I conducted on the Course. The description contains many qualities of a mystical experience. I asked her to write it down.

I was cooking for 2 years on an upper Mississippi towboat. One evening, after I had finished my evening chores, I was sitting on my bunk in my cabin on the towboat. I looked around at the furniture in the room and realized none of it was solid but made up of molecules with space in-between. I looked down at my hands and I saw the cells broken down into nucleus and all the spaciousness and then I disappeared!

I had no body, no boundaries. I was everywhere and nowhere. I was aware of a Peace that was so profound I knew it had never been shaken and never could be, without beginning or end.

I also had an Awareness of "All Knowledge." I Knew All Answers. I was also aware of the Unity of my Self with all people, animals and plants . . . even to a blade of grass. This seemed the most "natural" part of this experience. After reading "A Course in Miracles," I realized I had experienced a Holy Instant.

In a similar way, the Course, in speaking of what it calls "transformed vision," says:

> *The smallest leaf becomes a thing of wonder,*
> *and a blade of grass a sign of God's perfection.*

T-17.II.6:2–3

What is interesting about Bonnie's experience is the omniscient, all-knowing quality. This is true in so many instances, as with Eben Alexander, Anita Moorjani, and others.

There was a spot on the back of our farm where my mother, Milly, went when she could break free from all her responsibilities with my sister and I and our home. We were largely self-sufficient and it was Mother who made it that way. She was devoutly religious, reading the *Daily Word* each morning at her kitchen table. "I'll be sitting somewhere," she would say, "and I'll just float off. I always know when it's coming. I don't know where I go. It's not at all frightening." One day, she was sitting in the doctor's office when it happened, and the doctor told her that she died for a moment and then came back. She said these experiences were more real than ordinary life.

Mystical experiences often happen in an instant. Helen Schucman described the following experience, which she said happened in less than a minute on a subway in New York City in 1938, when she was twenty-nine years old. The following account is from her own words reported in Ken Wapnick's book about Helen, *Absence from Felicity*. Helen was riding a subway with her husband, Louis. The train was filled with people. "It smelled," she said, "like garlic and peanuts." A child with chocolate on his hands was patting his mother's face. Another mother was trying to wipe her child's vomit from her dress. Some men at one end of the train were arguing. Another child bent over and picked some chewing gum off the subway floor and put it in his mouth. Helen closed her eyes to shut out the scene.

And then a stunning thing happened. It was very brief. The intense emotions associated with it began to fade almost at once, and disappeared entirely in something less than a minute. An accurate account of what happened is impossible. As an approximation, however, I can say that it was as though a blinding light blazed up behind my closed eyes and filled my mind entirely. Without opening my eyes, I seemed to be watching a figure of myself as a child, walking directly into the light. The child seemed to know exactly what she was doing. It was as if the situation were completely familiar to her. For a moment she paused and knelt down, touching the shining ground with elbows, wrists, and forehead in what looked like an Eastern gesture of deep reverence.

Then she got up, walked to the right side and knelt again, this time resting her head as if leaning against a gigantic knee. The feeling of a great arm (one of "God's everlasting Arms") reached around her and she disappeared. The light grew even brighter, and I felt the most incredibly intense love stream from the light to me. It was so powerful that I literally gasped and opened my eyes.

I saw the light an instant longer, during which I loved everyone on the train with that same incredible intensity. Everyone there was unbelievably beautiful and incredibly dear.

DR. KENNETH WAPNICK, *ABSENCE FROM FELICITY,* PAGES 47, 48

Helen told her husband about her experience. He had read books on mysticism but he was more of a practical intellectual and he simply replied, "It is a common mystical experience; don't give it any more thought."

SECTION II

Holy Hell: The Account of a Visionary Journey

It is your world salvation will undo,
and let you see another world
your eyes could never find.

T-31.VI.3:4

FOUR

Prologue to the Journey

W hat appears next is a description of my own near-death experience. I've self-published this account three times before, in *Search for the Center* (1976), *Time, Death and A Course in Miracles* (1992), and *Missouri Mystic* (2003). This time I'm including what I'm calling a postmortem evaluation, along with this prologue, as with time and an enduring study of the Course, I've come to a better understanding of exactly what did happen.

This experience occurred in the jungles of Chiapas in southern Mexico in 1976. My friend, Shanti Rica Josephs, accompanied me on this journey and she went through a similar though different experience of her own. Shanti is a retired therapist living in New York City, sixteen years my senior, born on April 1, the same day as my mother. I have often thought of Shanti as my older sister. She has been for me an ever-wise adviser.

I met Shanti in 1972 through my then girlfriend, Edie Cadenhead. Edie was a gorgeous, petite blond, seven years older than I, a Gestalt psychologist and an actress in the soap opera *As the World Turns*. We met in a class I was teaching on Consciousness Expansion and Religious Experience at the New School University. Before long, we had fallen in love, and I moved in with Edie while retaining my office/apartment at General Theological Seminary.

In 1973, Edie rented out a bedroom within a brownstone she owned in New York City to a young woman named Marianne

Williamson, who would later become a prominent teacher of the Course. At the time, Marianne was trying to make it as a nightclub singer in New York City. Edie and I would go to hear her sing and clap extra loud to give her our support. Marianne and I would sit and have coffee in the morning and talk about the classes I was teaching. This was all pre-Course. Although I meet Helen and Bill in 1973, Helen did not formally introduce me to the Course until April 1975. By that time Marianne had moved on. Marianne would find the Course a few years later.

OUR GUIDE: SALVADOR ROQUET, MD

Early in 1976, Shanti asked me if I would like to go to Mexico that summer to meet Dr. Salvador Roquet, a Mexican psychiatrist and shaman. I immediately said, "Yes!" I didn't have to think about it. I was reading at the time *Journey to Ixtlan: The Lessons of Don Juan*, by Carlos Castaneda (1925–1998), the third in his series of books about his training under the tutelage of Don Juan Matus, a Yaqui "man of knowledge." His books provided fascinating descriptions of practices for increasing awareness and self-transformation. Several of his books (including *Journey to Ixtlan*) reached the *New York Times* bestseller list.

Life in itself is sufficient, self-explanatory and complete.
CARLOS CASTANEDA, *Journey to Ixtlan*

The experience took place under the supervision of Mexican psychiatrist, Dr. Salvador Roquet (1920–1995), and his colleagues. A man of love and compassion, Salvador was trained in the psychoanalytic tradition of Erich Fromm. Fromm served as professor at the National Autonomous University of Mexico in the early 1950s. There he established the psychoanalytic section of the medical school where Salvador received his training.

With time, Salvador became an eminent Mexican doctor. His responsibilities as a public health official brought him into contact with the Mexican Indians. In exchange for his help, the Indians taught him about the use of indigenous medicines in healing the mentally ill. In time, Salvador became a shaman, bringing together the disciplines of Western psychiatry and shamanism. He developed a way of helping us look at the ego—not to affirm its reality, but to help us understand its insanity and its ultimate nonexistence through the experience of nonego states.

Traditional talking therapy takes a long time—often many years—and then the patient may have only strengthened the ego, rather than overcoming it. Expose someone to death and see how the ego reacts. There is no faster way of getting to the truth. There are, of course, much gentler ways. Salvador's method blew open the door of my ordinary thinking and opened another dimension of reality that the body's eyes could never see. The Course then, more gently, showed me the meaning behind this experience and introduced a process that slowly led to an unwinding of the mind.

Salvador was a calm and gentle man. His peaceful presence was much like what I would discover in Ken Wapnick. Just being with Salvador gave one a sense of peace—like walking in a serene, Japanese garden. I always felt humbled in his presence, as did all those who worked with him. When he was not working with us directly, he could often be found reading the *Tao Te Ching*, the *Rigveda*, or a book of Sufi poetry. It was through Salvador that I developed a love for and began a study of the flute.

THE USE OF PSYCHEDELICS

Shanti and I made two trips into Mexico to work with Salvador, and on two different occasions he came to the United States, where we worked without psychedelics. We held workshops in New York and

Boston called "convivials." A convivial took place over the course of a weekend and involved keeping people awake until they "broke," at which point therapy began. On Friday evening, everyone's possessions (billfolds, watches, checkbooks, jewelry, and all accessories) were placed in large manila envelopes. The name of the owner was placed on the envelope, and the envelope was sealed, to be returned at the end of the weekend. The idea was to remove all external identities and get down to just being human beings. In the group sessions, no one was introduced by title or job description or given any distinction other than a first name.

At a convivial, various techniques were used to set the mood for therapy, including meditation, visualization, and the working through of emotions via music and slide show presentations. Eventually someone, weary from the lack of sleep and filled with emotions, would break. This opened the floodgates for others, and when the raw emotions were exposed, tears began to flow. Once the defenses were down and the masks began to fall away, the work began. The main task was one of helping people understand their "responsibility" in whatever they experienced.

On our first visit to Mexico, Shanti and I went into the jungles in Chiapas. On the second trip, we ventured into the Sierra Mazateca in Oaxaca to work with María Sabin and the native *Psilocybe* mushrooms.

> *If Heaven were outside you, you could not share in its gladness.*
> *Yet because it is within, the gladness, too, is yours.*

T-17.V.14:5–6

Psychedelics have been used for many thousands of years as a mechanism for leaving ordinary consciousness in order to perceive another dimension. There is no mention of an apple in the book of Genesis, and several anthropologists have suggested that the eating of forbidden fruit indicates early human's ingestion of some kind of psychedelic plant, a mushroom perhaps, that produced this altered awareness, in other words, a split mind. A quick survey of the Internet reveals hundreds of possible psychedelics. By providing changes in body chemistry, the ingesting of psychedelics allows a different way of "seeing." Psychedelics have for millennia been used as means for *waking from the dream* of earthly human life, by enabling us to *see* the dream.

The role plants play in the formation of early religion is well-documented. Indeed, the role of psychedelics in ritual can be traced to the beginnings of recorded history. R. Gordon Wasson has made a strong argument that the drink Soma (made from the *Amanita muscaria* mushroom), referred to in the *Rigveda* (the world's oldest scripture), was a means of reaching mystical experiences.

The Eleusinian and Dionysian rites of ancient Greece, which go back to as early as 1600 BCE, involved the use of a liquid that the participants drank prior to their initiation rites. Dr. Albert Hofmann (who first synthesized LSD in 1938 while working for the Sandoz pharmaceutical company in Basel, Switzerland) later wrote a book with R. Gordon Wasson titled, *The Road to Eleusis*, in which they showed that the drink Eleusinians drank was made from ergot, the dark parasitic fungus that grows on rye, which after dissolving in water has a chemical structure similar to that of LSD. Hofmann was the first person to isolate and name the principal psychedelic mushroom compound psilocybin.

FASTING

Fasting is a practice used in all of the world religious traditions as a means for internal cleansing and for opening to visionary experience and increased awareness. Fasting is recommended in the Old Testament book of Isaiah (58:8–9) so that "light will break forth from one's mind." Buddha fasted during some seven years before he had his experience of oneness under the Bodhi tree. Jesus fasted in the desert for some forty days before he began to hear the Voice for God. According to the Koran, Muhammad had been meditating several days alone in a cave when the angel Gabriel spoke to him, telling him to "Recite," and the Koran was given to him. In order to facilitate their spiritual experiences, early Christian church fathers ventured into the desert, where, isolated in caves away from the rest of the world, they, too, would fast to the point of near death and, thus, come to their visions. Fasting changes body chemistry as surely as does eating certain plants.

Near-death experiences inevitably involve an alteration in body chemistry. According to P.M.H. Atwater, the most commonly reported death experiences are those that occur during operations when one is under the influence of an anesthetic drug; when a body is completely traumatized, as in an automobile accident, war, drowning, or a host of other near-death ordeals; or during a severe illness, disease, high fever, loss of blood, or other trauma to the brain. While drugs like alcohol dull our senses, fasting, detox teas, and cleansing diets can heighten the senses. Although we may not be bodies, while we appear to be in them, it is hard to deny their *seeming* reality and the effect of physical experiences.

In 1993, when she was seventy-seven, my mother experienced a vision while having triple-bypass open-heart surgery and the replacement of her aorta with polyester tubing. After her operation, she told my sister, Ann, and me that she had been transported back to her hometown of Kirksville, Missouri. She said she had been gone for several days. She asked if I would take her back to Kirksville and the surrounding small towns to see some of the things she saw in this vision. There, she said, she had ventured into a cave where she saw and talked to her deceased mother, father, sisters, and other relatives.

OFF TO THE JUNGLE

Shanti and I flew to Mexico City, where we met Salvador and his family of fourteen children; David, an American potter from Tennessee, and his wife, Linda; Frank, a balding, bearded psychologist from San Francisco; Rick, a long, lanky intellectual assistant to Salvador; and two other assistants. They would all venture with us into the jungle. Every moment with Salvador we were in training, even though we didn't always know it. The journey was not just about what was going to happen when we got into the jungle. Salvador did everything deliberately, all the while preparing us for our climatic awakening. Only later did I realize how carefully he executed every detail of our awakening.

We drove as far as we could into the jungle in a caravan of three cars. I drove a Volkswagen Beetle with Shanti, David, and Linda. Our destination was an Indian pueblo somewhere in Chiapas, a two-day drive from Mexico City. The first day we stopped and spent the night in a charming hotel with an open courtyard decorated with fountains and flowers. Unlike my hometown of Mexico, Missouri, with the courthouse in the center of the square, this Mexican town's central plaza was dominated by a large Catholic cathedral in the center, surrounded by a park a block long and a block wide. On the outside of the park, along the sidewalk, people were selling local produce and handicrafts laid out on blankets under a canopy.

The next morning, we visited an Indian museum, and I bought an Indian flute. Then we took off. The lead driver, one of Salvador's assistants, drove with keen resolve and far too fast—as though we had to reach our destination at a certain time. That evening, as we were racing down the dusty street of a Mexican village, a scrawny-looking dog stepped out of the dust of the car ahead of me and sacrificed his life in front of my eyes. I hit the brakes—there was a yelp, a quick, dull thud, and a mess of fur, blood, and broken bones in the dust behind us. In a fraction of a second, an impression of the red eyes of the dog staring at the headlights of the car was burned in my mind. He had stopped, turned, and looked at me a second before I hit him. It was the first death that day.

We arrived at about eleven p.m. at our destination, a combination cantina, pool hall, and butcher house. Exhausted from continually driving roads that had become progressively rougher, dirtier, and dustier, we reached the cantina just in time to witness the slaughtering of a cow, the culminating experience of our evening. Though I did not realize it until later, it was all part of Salvador's plan. He wanted us to witness this death, and the Indians had waited for our arrival before the butchering began.

Tied up outside the cantina, where we were going to spend the night, was the poor cow, her eyes wide with terror, mooing and pulling on a rope tied to a tree. She knew her fate. Beyond this spot there were no more electric lights or refrigeration. To provide themselves with meat, once a fortnight, the natives butchered a cow. They began when the air was cool and worked through until morning. As a young boy, I had watched the butchering of pigs and beef cows. I enjoyed the camaraderie of farmers coming together to share in a mutual task. After butchering, everyone shared in the spoils. Everyone who helped got to take something home and the owner of the cow always got the best part.

Now we were sharing with Mexican Indians in their night of slaughter. Beyond insects and mice, I could not kill anything, and I didn't care to see anything killed. Shanti was, as with all things, fascinated with what was about to happen. "Oh, wow! Look at that!"

Standing looking into the face of the doomed cow, an Indian stepped forward and placed a large pan near her throat. Then another Indian walked forward and quickly cut her throat. She began to moo, an awful, woeful wail of death, as blood shot out partly into the pan, partly splashing out of the pan, making a puddle of mud in the dusty earth, forcing us to jump back lest we became splattered with mud and blood. A few minutes later, weak from loss of blood, the cow fell on her front knees, then over on the ground. She kicked her legs a few times with a violent jerk. The last delayed, surprise kick tripped one of the Indians who got too close. The cow stopped moving. She was dead.

All night long, the Indians hacked, slashed, hewed, and sawed the carcass of the cow—talking, making jokes, drinking tequila, and spitting on the ground. A dirty white sheet drawn across a wire was all that separated our sleeping quarters from their butchering. On the sheet, we could see their shadows hacking, sawing, and joking the night away. Exhausted as we were, it was impossible to sleep. Salvador alone had the privilege of crawling up on top of the pool table. There he lay sound asleep like a baby—adding to the cacophony and tormenting us by snoring all night. I couldn't get the image of the poor cow with her terrified eyes out of my mind. And then there were mosquitoes, mosquitoes, and more mosquitoes eating us like the specialty of the day.

Early the next morning, Indian women arrived, carrying on their heads large empty blue-and-white-speckled enamel pans, which they filled with the meat. Covering their pans with cloth to keep the flies off the meat, they started their march back to their homes in the jungle. Lacking refrigeration, they would cook the meat as soon as they returned. When it ran out, they would go without meat or rely on local game until the next butchering.

Up and packed, we were treated to a meal of *huevos con frijoles*—eggs with beans—and coffee. There was no lunch or dinner. We would not eat again until we returned from the jungle. We were off, riding on top of our backpacks and luggage in the back of bullock carts. Salvador took us to a safe space where no one would happen upon us. Our destination: an island in the jungle surrounded by a swamp, where the only decent means of transportation was bullock cart.

The hut on the island looked a good bit like the chicken coops on our farm, though our chickens may have fared better. There was one room with a wooden floor and a porch. Though we were hungry and on edge from a lack of sleep the night before, this was going to be *the* night. There was no delay. Salvador's plan was to keep us on edge. Before the night was over, we were going *over* the edge.

Ever the doctor, Salvador checked everyone's blood pressure. He had never lost anyone and wasn't going to now. We would each go into the experience about half an hour apart. I went first. First we were given a tab of pure Sandoz LSD under the tongue. We then lay down on our sleeping bags, our eyes completely covered with a black sleep mask, which was covered, in turn, by a bandana to exclude all possible light. External stimulation was to be kept to a minimum. The objective was inner sight. Earphones covered our ears and Salvador had an extensive collection of tapes, tape record-ers, mixers, and enough batteries to provide us with the sounds that would carry us through the night.

About half an hour into the experience, after the LSD began to take its full effect and we were flying off into a beautiful psyche-delic world, we each received an intramuscular shot of ketamine. Ketamine is a highly effective anesthetic, as it does not interfere with the autonomic systems of breathing or heartbeat. It is used with animals, and it is often used in emergency surgery and in bat-tlefield operations. It is *the* anesthetic of choice when ventilation equipment is not available, and it is often used in operations on children. Ketamine is a very powerful muscle relaxant, so much so that the body simply passes out, and you cannot move. Ketamine is also a psychedelic, and so *wide-awake*, on LSD, the mind cannot pass out—though the body is a goner. With the body completely immobile and the mind ten thousand times more awake than ever, you cannot hold on to the body identity. Ketamine both accelerated and smoothed the trip.

Several years later a post-op nurse told me that when someone has received ketamine it is clearly marked on his or her chart, as people who are awakening from an operation in which they have had ketamine often report having been on a trip. They have gone places, visited other dimensions, seen unbelievable things.

With earphones covering our ears, Salvador controlled the mix of music, chanting, drum beating, flute playing, and other sounds that came our way. Early on came the stentorian sound of the Balinese "Ramayana Monkey Chant" or "Kecak," the sound of a trance ritual accompanied by a chorus of some 150 men. (Watch it on YouTube.) It provided a fascinating experience of one-mindedness. Somewhere in the middle of the experience, there was a long-looping cycle of *Boléro*, the one-movement orchestral piece by composer Maurice Ravel. The climax, what I called "the Voice for God," came during the most beautiful Gregorian chants sung by Trappist monks. No one was allowed to touch us. This was to be a totally inward, non-external experience. The objective was inner sight. No one would talk to you, and you were so far gone that talking would have been impossible anyway.

INFINITELY MORE REAL

In the experience that followed, I saw something I have always sought, and for a moment *re-membered*. I do not expect it to be comprehensible in ordinary terms. I present it as a phenomenological experience worthy of examination. If you cannot accept it as fact, think of it as a dream, a vision, or a hallucination. There are some dreamlike qualities to this experience, particularly the way in which various scenes seem to morph from one into another.

My encounter, however, was very vivid, "infinitely more real" than what we call "everyday life." This is a universal characteristic of those who have near-death experiences. As Dr. Eben Alexander said in his memoir, *Proof of Heaven*, "Though I didn't know where I was or even *what* I was, I was absolutely sure of one thing: this place I'd suddenly found myself in was completely real. The word *real* expresses something abstract, and it's frustratingly ineffective at conveying what I'm trying to describe." One difference between what I am about to describe and what sometimes happens in other near-death experiences is the dissolution of the ego, or personal sense of self. Many near-death experiences describe the ego and the personality of the individual as still intact during and after the experience. Many go through a tunnel, visit deceased relatives, have conversations with enlightened beings, and then are told they must return. There is often no *trauma* over having lost a body, but that was not true in my experience.

To speak of "my ego" is a strange use of words, as there is in reality no ego, so the ego can only be spoken of as a mythological character. In any event, "my ego," this *temporal identity*, was not left intact, and I endured sensations so immeasurably rich that the beginning phases of this event were absolutely terrifying. When the ego runs up against death, when there is no question about it, when the "jig is up," it can be horrifying. In this experience, it became clear that what we call "human consciousness" is only a tiny speck of awareness, and consciousness itself is a basic cosmic phenomenon related to the organization of energy. During this experience, I achieved a level of attention that occurs in emergency situations where one's life is in peril. It is similar to that which Zen master, Yasutani Roshi, uses in his description of *shikantaza* in Zen meditation:

> Let's imagine that you are engaged in a duel of swordsmanship of the kind that used to take place in ancient Japan. As you face your opponent, you are unceasingly watchful, set, ready. Were you to relax your vigilance even momentarily, you would be cut down instantly. A crowd gathers to see the fight. Since you are

not blind, you see them from the corner of your eye, and since you are not deaf, you hear them. But not for an instant is your mind captured by these sense impressions.

A whole new language appeared, the words of which I've tried to render into English with italics. It includes a few new words and combinations of words. Although this experience sounds painful, and it was, the lasting effect has been quite positive. A door that had been closed was opened, and it cannot ever again be completely closed. My life since has been an attempt to move ever deeper into an understanding of what happened. No tool in this search has been more helpful or provided more clarity than *A Course in Miracles*.

FIVE

The Experience Itself

THE BEGINNING—THE LOSS OF BODY

The following description is written in the present tense, as that is the way I experienced it—instantaneous, immediately, and intimately.

At first there is nothing but a sense of peace, followed by a growing sense of expansion and then a growing apprehension. Then suddenly a massive expansion. My arms come back over my head; my heels dig into the earth below me. My whole body arches itself upward; energy pours though my arms and legs as huge arcing lights meet in the center, then pour back in a myriad of different colors. I experience what I can only describe as an orgasm in every cell, a super-sensational edge cutting through everything. Thick juice pours from my being, while intense emotions pass through me. I tell myself that I can hold on, that I can hold on, that I can . . . but I cannot. I'm face-to-face with something uncontrollable and irreversible—a chain reaction tearing apart every aspect of being.

Any identity I might have had is being *ripped* away. There is nothing I can do to hold on to any form of ordinary reality. The pain is intense, immense, and I'm completely insane. In one final arch, with thousands of volts of energy running through me, I let go of the body completely. I simply cannot hold on any longer. I say, "I'm dead." I'm quite dead. The acceptance comes not casually but as a firm and clear fact. Salvador, beautiful Salvador, my savior, has made a horrible mistake: he has accidentally killed one of his students. My body is now a lifeless piece of clay and I have no attachment to it.

Antimatter and the Collapse of Time

I'm being pulled by immense energies, pivoted back and forth through a whip-like motion from a convex into a concave arch. Outwardly I'm shot forward, while inwardly I'm pulled backward faster and faster—like a logarithmic spiral—exponentially increasing speed with every step, becoming infinitely smaller as the universe opens to its maximum. Everything keeps expanding outward and then collapsing inward. I'm left with a kaleidoscopic vision in which "I" (whatever that is) am watching cells divide, and I'm part of it. There is an inward turning—a point of condensation—then suddenly a burst, a shot forward, and a whole new world is present. The only term I can think of to describe this is *matter-antimatter*.

Time collapses in a series of violent jerks. My life, my past, are disappearing—all dying—turning to dust. For a moment, I remember Daddy, my life on the farm, and that oh-so-ordinary reality that seems like a space of bliss. I feel the most incredible sense of connection with the earth and that man, and then I experience what I call the severing of the *genetic-ego*. The earth and every aspect of it flashing before me are then burned into a tiny crisp and disappear in a zigzagging line that delineates a new universe. A web or grid now defines a new, very familiar universe. In fact, this is the most familiar thing there is. This is where we all are. This is Home. This is where we all always have been.

As you approach the Beginning,
you feel the fear of the destruction of your thought system
upon you as if it were the fear of death.

T-3.VII.5:10

The Fear of Death and the Collapse of the Ego

Again, I remember my ordinary identity and the brief statement I made in life. Then something says, "Oh, yeah! Jon Mundy." Then there is a giggle, a roll of laughter, and I see how puny and insignificant that identity was. My striving, my worrying and working through problems, were all suddenly absurd—even funny.

There occurs now an element that is truly difficult to describe, a point of absolute insanity, in which the ego judges itself to death. This seeming reality is then seared, stamped out, excluded from existence. It is not that I become unconscious. *Something* becomes far, far more conscious than ever. The self I had created, however, is burned, not because it is bad, but simply because Jon Mundy, as I had known him, was unreal—or meaningless. Like a pair of old pants no longer needed, whatever that identity was is now tossed away.

Descent into Hell—The Experience of a Star

I become aware of myself as a tiny point in the tail of a gigantic star, whirling itself toward the center of something, a single *point-of-consciousness*, of *consciousness . . . feeling . . . knowledge . . .* nothing more than a tiny subsection of the continuum of something immense. I scream at the enormity of what is ahead, completely incapable of resisting the force that pulls me forward. I am experiencing a complete deflagration. The sensation is that of pure and raging firepower. I am part of an incredible network of other *points-of-consciousness* on the tip of the tail of a star somewhere in some space, hurling itself toward the center of something.

I understand with complete empathy the *thought-feeling* of every other point in this tail. I will give anything to stop this experience. I have nothing to give. Each of these *points-of-consciousness* is screaming for the experience to stop, pleading for forgiveness for having *mistaken-themselves*, begging for just one little moment of death, rest, and unconscious nonexistence—my own voice drowning in this cacophony. Caught in this cosmic maelstrom, unable to resist the intense gravity, I'm pulled relentlessly into its center.

The Merging of Multiple Minds

Everything stops. There is absolute silence. The pain ceases. Nothing is happening—just some kind of pure, nonjudgmental awareness: looking. Perhaps something like the awareness of a baby. Turning inside out on myself, I focus down into a sphere surrounded by other spheres, all of which are *coming-moving-away-from-me*. I'm now merging with other forms of consciousness. At first I think it is the consciousness of the people on earth whom I have known and loved, but it is also the consciousness of those I have *always* known and now *re-membered*. I cannot identify this consciousness as human. There is no singular ego consciousness, rather a much broader perspective with incredible depth of perception. As a grain of wheat is ground into flour, excited with leavening, and then turned into bread, so is my ego crushed, and then my mind opened into a new but very familiar *merging of multiple minds*.

The New Vision

I'm seeing the way I imagine a computer might see. Everything is divided into tiny cubic forms, each, in turn, divided into innumerable cubic forms ad infinitum, each a certain depth of space, each a certain gradation of color, running in all directions, forming an immense array of patterns. I can see in a complete 360 degrees and *see-feel* each space of depth in descending gradations, and focus a kind of telescopic vision that comes down on, or opens up to, larger visions with amazing rapidity. The colors of these other spheres run from deep black on the outside down through dark then light red, blues, and yellows, with blinding red, yellow, or blue centers—the colors all perfectly clear, as there is no atmosphere that separates me from my perception. There are sounds, too—the music of the spheres, beyond the best of our symphonies; the music is absolutely indescribable. Everywhere energy pulsates through everything, undulation upon undulation. Nothing is constant; everything is moving.

The Language of This World

The language of this world is beautiful, clear, precise, exact, melodic— a kind of *musical-equation*. It is difficult to say whether the language aspect predominated over the *math-music* or the *math-music* over the language. All language has melted and merged into one language, a language that, strangely enough, I can understand more clearly than English or any earthly sound. I could not only hear but also *see* elaborate expressions produced in beautiful, four-dimensional geometric design like the whole of the Universe was speaking.

Like a Möbius strip, ideas turn into form, then back into ideas. I'm *seeing-reality-as-it-is*, yet not seeing—but *knowing*. The sophistication with which everything fits together is truly beyond belief. There simply are no accidents, no coincidences. Each *musical-equation* is an exact and melodically logical statement that gives rise to paradoxes and results in emotional sensations. Some, I sense, are the names of authors of complicated formulas, already determined by previous generations of perfected consciousness.

The Marketplace

A *musical equation* defines the world, and once expressed, produces the experiences endured. Complicated emotional states are being "called out" by spheres from different directions. There occurs now a point-counterpoint, back-and-forth play of *math-musical-equation-points*, each produced in rapid-fire order so that a marketplace effect occurs as each *point-of-consciousness* calls out for various programs to be played, or responds to programs being played in another part of the galaxy. An explosion or burning of some great equation, system of belief, or personality sends *A-wake* through the other spheres, causing us to *pay-attention*.

Insight flashes upon insight, flashes upon insight. With every conclusion, I become aware of a position that stands in opposition to that conclusion, and a third position that stands between these two and, thus, becomes a new conclusion. Each of these *concluding-equations* can then be *swallowed* by a *checkmating-concluding-equation*, which then might be burned into a tiny cinder to become an *old-truth* in a *greater-realization*. I or any other *point-of-consciousness* might call out an equation that predominates in value over the last conclusion. Visually, the experience is like looking down a kaleidoscope—watching everything fall into the middle, each old form falling off to the side, while new beauty is ever left before me.

My relationship to the other *points-of-consciousness* depends upon who is playing the program, whether I'm being pulled toward some other program, whether the program seems pleasant or unpleasant. I try, under the elaboration of some hypothesis, to gain some temporary control, but soon wander into a *negative-deviation* and am instantly swallowed by a *checkmating-evaluating-equation*.

Your one central problem has already been answered
and you have no other.

W-80:1:2

For every decision I make, I'm congratulated for having reached the right conclusion—then shown the paradoxical nature of my decision. I then find myself standing over a new proposition that makes my original position seem so inconsequential that I'm sure I have erred, even though it is clear that I have chosen quite rightly—indeed, the only way I could have chosen. It is clear that I have made the right decision, which is wrong. That is, I cannot help but make the right decision, even when it is the wrong one. Each time this happens, I roll over and turn out another way. Each change of form brings a new perception and a new identity, which I begin to grasp, only to lose it to another form. It is very hard to know what is having this experience.

I don't know how to control my thoughts in the presence of what I perceive are Divine beings who long ago figured out what I'm just now seeing. I grasp only bits and pieces of this alternate reality, which I'm now attempting to convey on these pages. Other parts I remember momentarily in intuitive flashes—holy instances in which I see again a tiny piece of this puzzle obscured by a misty cloud. For a time, in the midst of this experience, it seems I knew all that is to be known—all of it. There was then nothing but Love.

Later I conclude that I knew nothing. I had become *too conscious* and knew no way not to be. An atomic explosion is going on in consciousness, always has been and will be. For a moment, I gain the ultimate insight into the absurdity of the universe and think I shall never be able to return to that merciful self-deception that is necessary for what we call sanity or society. I wanted to die, but that is impossible—the mind cannot die. The more consciousness knows of itself, the more impossible it is to know anything about its origin. There is no past—no place of beginning.

There is no past or future, and the idea of birth into a body
has no meaning either once or many times.

M-24.2

Life *is* thought. Life simply is and always will be. In this incredible world, every thought is instantly turned into form; every defective form is burned; every perfect form turned yet again into higher perfection. I have no idea if I will ever return to bodily life. There is clearly no choice or chance of ever leaving. There is only fantastic *energy-information-flow.*

God wills you learn what always has been true:
that He created you as part of Him,
and this must still be true because ideas leave not their source.

T-26.VII.13:2

THE PULL OF GOD

From the "northeast" section of consciousness comes a holy sound (glorious Gregorian chanting). As I focus on it, the pitch gets louder, almost deafening. God, it seems, is behind that sound, but it is impossible to go that way, as the gravitational pull of the universe before me is even more intense. I further think that by following such a path, I shall lose an even greater hold on consciousness, which means going crazy faster, but it is impossible to go crazy any faster than I already am.

I would do anything to have something that is real in the old and ordinary sense of the term. I call out several times for Judy (my girlfriend at the time of this experience and now a forever friend).

Love is the only thing that makes sense. But I had left far behind that speck of dust on which I at one time lived in some more unconscious and more naive condition. Earth is dumb and stupid, and I want to be dumb and stupid. What bliss, what joy it would be to return to my *animal-body*.

Throwing Up and the Burning of Karma

I say, "shit," "*merde*," and "goddamn it," in every language I know and many I do not. The sensation is like throwing up awful pieces of sandy green slime. This gives me a sense of relief. I feel clearer and more centered. While riding the tail end of the star, I beg for forgiveness, which is not forthcoming and, it seems, undeserved, but I could not help begging for it. By saying something like *mistake-myself*, I beg to be released from *the-sin-of-desiring-ego*. After this experience, I read a dialogue between Oscar Ichazo (known for the Enneagram of Personality) and Dr. John Lilly (known for communicating with dolphins), in which they discuss this effect as the *burning-of-one's-karma*. I now realize that no darkness within is ever able to hide. There is also nothing I want to hide, and I joyfully accept my fate.

Coming to Consciousness

I'm beginning to "descend" back into form. I'm falling back toward the earth—going through stages, each stage morphing from one into another. I am a tip on the peak of a high mountain. Dirt and rocks are falling off the sides as I begin to *fall* into form. I'm turning into a temple; then I'm on a couch within the temple, surrounded by millions of other *points-of-consciousness*. Those close to me are beginning to take on humanoid form and begin to back away. Other points, less humanoid and more distant, begin to move more slowly. They, too, are increasing their level of awareness. I call upon them to pay attention and tell them that they will be relieved of ignorance and pain. This returns a sense of ego, along with a sudden sense of power—and then intense loneliness.

I think that these other *points-of-consciousness* will have to come to awareness, just as I have. They will have to go through the same pain, and that seems so horrible. Yet it is clear that, when one breaks through, there is less pain. Furthermore, it is clear that I am in want of greater wisdom, and I sink down into denser form. This is a great relief, at least, though still far from what life used to be.

Regaining Ego and the Expression of Anger

Finally, by getting a hold of my vocal cords, I'm able to scream, "*Stop it, stop it, stop it!*" and "*Wait a minute, wait a minute, wait a minute.*" Recovering vocal cords means I am able to return somewhat to bodily life, although I have yet to return to flesh and bones—my molecules still spread out over immense space. Desperate to obtain some form of identity, I gain control over an arm, and I move it around in front of me. As I do, the air gives way in millions of points of rarefied sensation.

I exert more energy, and the world backs farther away with caution. I gain some control, but it is momentary; then I immediately see my error and begin to sink into lower form. Now when I bring my arms up over my body, it is possible to tear away an outer layer of consciousness, as one might strip away an outer layer of a cocoon.

I'm now *coming-to-consciousness* in a large circular room. The walls all around are padded with different colored blocks—something one could bump into without hurting oneself. I'm not in ordinary human form. I'm more like a cocoon of energy—more like some kind of embryo. Around me are a number of human beings—including my former girlfriend, Edie. (Edie died in 1989 at the age of only fifty-one. She was very much in her body at the time of this experience.) Most notable is one young man who keeps saying, "Do you want to get up?" which meant did I want to wake up, or be reborn in this other world?

I am experiencing this *coming-to-consciousness* as a formidable *ignitiation* (an initiation by fire), in which I am being introduced to higher knowledge in an advanced stage of the future. I'm being born again, not the way a baby is born, but the way a concept is born or a cocoon unraveled; more and more clearly I see the truth of the world about me. I'm an embryo developing very rapidly—incapable of stopping the development. There is a lot of excitement about my birth. Edie and my other friends, the ones I've known forever, are there to greet me, and they laughingly smile upon my *ignitiation* and welcome me to a higher stage they have already attained. But I can't pull through. I cannot remove the veil. I let go of my struggle and sink down into a less conscious but again more peaceful state.

An Ape Scientist

I'm now *coming-to-consciousness* as an ape-scientist. I think I'm one of the first people ever to come to consciousness. Then there is a sudden pang of guilt, the thought that something has gone wrong. I'm Adam on the first morning of awakening, and I am alone in my thinking. When I realize what is happening, I beg the others to stop their own endeavors and rest for a moment, for we are very near the truth, and if we go more quickly, we will find ourselves passing right through the truth to a new form of insanity that surpasses our present state of stupidity. But now it seems it's too late, and I begin to cry out, "Who's the doctor?" Who is unleashing this atomic reaction? Who is cracking this cosmic egg and unleashing these molecules of mind?

Time

The next part of this description is very important. I can only say that I am convinced that I have *already-not-yet-had* this experience in the *future-past*. Yet, I'm so in the present that the concepts of past and future have lost their significance. Perhaps I had this experience in some nightmare before I was born, certainly in some state of *unconscious-madness*—a state to which I shall have to return, to which I am even now returning, through a black hole in space, through a tunnel in time, in which everything is turned inside out on itself. Now I understood what Nietzsche meant by *eternal recurrence*. The future, like the past, pulsates, undulates, spirals, and turns over and over again. Everything is happening in a radically loaded *now*. One single thought released forever into eternity, ever breaking itself into repeatedly more complex forms, ever being burned, burning, and being born again.

Responsibility

I am responsible for this experience, because I am there. To accept responsibility for an irreversible chain reaction in consciousness is immense. Yet I'm back. I'm home. I'm in the place I always have been. My external and now lost life is a story into which I escaped in time. Time is phenomenal because it is sequential. Events seem to happen one after another, and because of that, they are comprehensible. We live in time to learn a lesson, one I had not yet learned at the time of this experience—one I am still learning. Ever since, I've wanted to find out what happened; I've been trying to *re-member*.

Sufficiently back into my body to be able to move, I get hold of a brass crucifix. Though remarkably porous, it provides a sense of solidity in my hand. It is something to hang on to. Its symbolic quality means nothing, and I scream, "Who the hell is Jesus?" Perhaps he had something of this experience thousands of years ago. But that information is of little use in this moment.

I pray then, although I know not to what god, that this experience will never have to happen to anyone else. Yet, it seems that innumerable other worlds, or *points-of-consciousness*, were—or better, *are*—having the experience in much the same way that I did. I know now that the whole experience was correlated to my own state of being; therefore, what I saw, another might not see, nor do I believe it is necessary for anyone else to have the same experience. I was going through something clearly beyond my level of perception and emotional preparedness. I was seeing a universe so much beyond this one that there was nothing left of this world at all, save perhaps atoms, molecules, asteroids, comets, and stars of deepest space—intelligent beings far more intelligent than a poor human mind could comprehend.

I am to that world what an ant is to this one—only more so. I'm totally at the mercy of that world. An ant that turns its head up into the light and sees a gigantic being standing above it cannot possibly know what that being is. The light, the sound, the whole of that world above (which I know is within), is totally overwhelming, so much so that all my ordinary ego defenses collapse in the face of it. What lights a mystic's way blinds an ordinary man, unprepared for the light of knowledge.

Return to the Body

I return to the body completely dumbfounded. I can hardly believe I have reintegrated myself into an old and familiar body. For the next two hours, I can only sit and look at my right hand. I cannot believe I am back in my body. My ordinary mind is wide-awake, and I'm completely exhausted.

It's a long time before I'm able to talk again. Words seem so physical, so dumb, so inadequate and inconsequential. When I can talk a little, Salvador begins to ask me questions about what happened. He encourages me to describe as much as possible, and he asks me to write it down.

Back in New York a few days later, I sat down at a typewriter. The internal tongue was loosened, and what I've reported came back as I just described it, but I must tell you that I translated this experience though the framework of the human brain and wrote it with human hands. You, the reader, see it with human eyes or hear it with human ears and translate it through your own thought system. Therefore, you gather only the smallest glimpse of what happened. I have painted a picture of a possibility for consciousness—the description of a world hundreds of thousands of times more real, more focused, immediate, intense, expansive, and all-inclusive—than this one.

Did I Die?

I thought that I did. There are some who say I did not. My heart was still beating as I lay there in that hut in that sleeping bag, my eyes covered with a sleep mask and a bandana. I have both heard and read accounts by others who have gone through similar experiences with Salvador. Every one describes it as a death experience, including the dissolution of the ego. I had no idea the experience was going to be as completely shattering as it was. If I had, I might not have done it. I thought it might be like my first experience with LSD back in 1966, but it was more—much more. I went through this experience several times in the years in which I worked with Salvador. I remember this first time in more detail because of the ego's encounter with death.

I remember very little of later experiences. By then, when I saw what was coming, I just ran and jumped off the cliff. I just let go, surrendered to the experience, and disappeared. So the other, later experiences, I don't remember, except for the very beginning and a bit of the return back into the body. This was especially true for my 2007 near-death encounter with encephalitis. The Course says that the one thing we have not truly done is that we have not *truly* forgotten our bodies. For a few moments, I didn't just forget my body; I lost it.

> *The internal dialogue is what grounds people in the daily world.*
> *The world is such and such or so and so,*
> *only because we talk to ourselves about its being such*
> *and such and so and so.*
> *The passageway into the world of shamans opens up*
> *after the warrior has learned to shut off his internal dialogue.*

CARLOS CASTANEDA, THE WHEEL OF TIME: THE SHAMANS OF MEXICO, THEIR THOUGHTS ABOUT LIFE, DEATH AND THE UNIVERSE

SHUTTING OFF THE INTERNAL DIALOGUE

A truly overwhelming experience can shut down the ego mind's internal dialogue. This shutting down of the mind's internal self-talk or babble, is the purpose of meditation; it is also the intention of the Course. How can we learn if we can't be quiet long enough to to listen? The Course is gentle. It *coaxes* rather than *forces* us into silence and receptivity. We simply cannot hear the Voice for God when there is a lot of mind static going on. I was forced into silence, as my mind was literally blown apart and I was left sitting there in bewilderment holding the pieces and trying to understand what had happened. I do not recommend that anyone do what Shanti and I did. Let your journey be gentle.

SIX

Postmortem

Enlightenment must come little by little,
otherwise it would overwhelm.

IDRIES SHAH (1924–1996), SUFI MYSTIC

Mystical experiences may fade, but they are never completely forgotten. Salvador asked Shanti, myself, and all of the participants to engage in a *deliberate* recall in order to deepen our memories of what we had experienced—similar to purposefully recalling a dream in order to see more elements within the dream. What I lived through was like a very rapid dream—somewhat like the camera moving constantly in the film *Birdman*, only much more rapidly.

Our experiences happened in the years 1976, 1977, and 1978. I have had no similar experiences since that time and feel no need to do so. After the last experience, Salvador asked me a question, and while I don't remember the question, I do remember my response. I said, "I'm already dead," to which he replied, "You don't have to do this anymore." And I never did.

Back in New York, I met with Helen, Ken, and Judy Whitson at Judy's apartment in The Beresford apartment building in New York City. There, I read them the account of this experience. The account confirms many of the things the Course says—that we are not bodies, that there is no death or time, and that we are making up this world.

No one remains in hell,
for no one can abandon his Creator,
nor affect His perfect, timeless and unchanging Love.
You will find Heaven.

W-131.5:1–2

The first part of my experience was hellish because of the tremendous resistance I had in letting go of an identity I thought was real, a personality—a form of individuality which I had constructed in a short 33 years of living in a body and a dream containing no lasting reality. Those who have had similar experiences understand the profundity *of the reality* of what was seen. The good news is that *we all already know this.* It *is* after all, our eternal reality. Being trapped within the framework of the ego, the world remains a dream of time and death from which we are yet to awaken. We all want to awaken and we are each of us making our way Home. Hopefully helping each other along the way. That's the only way.

Out, out, brief candle!
Life's but a walking shadow,
a poor player that struts and frets
his hour upon the stage and is heard no more.
It is a tale told by an idiot,
full of sound and fury, signifying nothing.

WILLIAM SHAKESPEARE, MACBETH, ACT 5, SCENE 5

After I found myself wanting to tell people that they were not bodies but soon I saw the futility in it. No one could understand what I was talking about. One friend even asked me to stop telling people they were not bodies. I was, however, a minister, I had a pulpit, and I was officiating at lots of funerals, so I began to speak of what I had seen–trying not to scare folks with the hellish part, and out of concern about people's phobic reactions avoiding talking about the psychedelics.

The body seems so obvious; and it is so consistently promoted as our "reality" and seen by us as the essence of life that it's hard to see what seems to be "the most real" thing is in fact not real at all. The mere mortality of the body is proof of the non-existence of the body. The body is born and then dies. Just like a light it is turned on and then with time it burns out. It has no eternity in it.

> *Do not project this fear to time,*
> *for time is not the enemy that you perceive.*
> *Time is as neutral as the body is,*
> *except in terms of what you see it for.*
>
> T-26.VIII.3:6

Both the body and time are neutral. They are both tools given to us to aid in the journey Home. Time and the body can be given over to God or the ego. The choice is simple. Which way shall we choose to go?

We all know that we are not a body. Yet, our greatest fear is that one day we will lose our bodies. The ego keeps us attached to the body. Sometimes when someone dies another will say, "It's so awful." It is not awful at all, though certainly it is heartbreaking to those who now have empty places in their home and their lives, who no longer can share with that person in space/time.

> *The acceptance of the Atonement by everyone is only a matter of*
> *time. This may appear to contradict free will*
> *because of the inevitability of the final decision, but this is not so.*
> *You can temporize and you are capable of enormous procrastination,*
> *but you cannot depart entirely from your Creator,*
> *Who set the limits on your ability to miscreate.*
>
> T-2.III.3:1–3

The experience enabled me to see that all of our problems have already been solved. Indeed, all our problems are surface realities that cover greater problems of trust, openness, and faith. How easy it is to see the surface realities, the petty difference in opinions that bind us and tie us in knots. These are the things to be thrown off and tossed way. Freeing one's being from these judgments and prejudices gives rise to feelings of purity, cleanliness, and innocence.

> *It is true, just as you fear, that to acknowledge*
> *Him is to deny all that you think you know.*
> *But what you think you know was never true.*

T-16.II.6:6-7

A good deal of my experience was hellish because I was unprepared to handle it. Had I had greater faith, say, to follow "the Voice of God," during the singing of the *Gregorian Chants*, I am sure the experience would have been even more profound; but it was already more profound than I could endure. I was sure that if I followed *the Sound of God,* I would disappear. Now I know that that is true, only the ego would disappear and the loss of the ego is the loss of nothing. Since the experience, I've had much more respect for schizophrenia.

> *Schizophrenia is one of the forms in which,*
> *often through quite ordinary people,*
> *the light begins to break through*
> *the cracks in our all-too-closed minds.*

R.D. LAING, SCOTTISH PSYCHIATRIST

The good thing about the Course is that it helps us deal with our madness now, enabling us to awaken slowly and, thus, without going insane. I actually went temporarily insane, a fact which I later found confirmed by Jungian psychologist, Marie-Louise Von Franz:

. . . a schizophrenic episode is often prepared by dreams of
world destruction. In modern terms it is generally an atomic
explosion, or the end of the world, the stars fall down—
absolutely apocalyptic images. This generally announces that the
consciousness of this human being is in a state of explosion or is
going to explode and his reality awareness will soon disappear.

MARIE-LOUISE VON FRANZ, CREATION MYTHS (1972)

This is exactly what happened. My reality awareness as I had come to know it—as an ego being on planet Earth—disappeared, and I was left with another reality that ". . . *(my) eyes could never find.*"

What seems eternal all will have an end.
The stars will disappear, and night and day will be no more.
All things that come and go, the tides, the seasons and the lives of
men; all things that change with time
and bloom and fade will not return.

T-29.VI.2:7–9

There are those who say that what Salvador put us through was not kind. It was, however, the hammer needed to break the ego's hardened shell.

Madness need not be a breakdown.
It may also be a break-through.

R.D. LAING, SCOTTISH PSYCHIATRIST

When I was in college and then again when I was in seminary I took a class titled, *The Psychology of Religion.* Our textbook in both cases was *The Psychology of Religion* by Walter Houston Clark, Ph.D., Professor of the Psychology of Religion at Andover Newton Theological School in Massachusetts and a former Dean at Hartford Seminary. Dr. Clark and I were to later meet through Spiritual Frontiers in New York, and for both of us, it was like meeting a long lost friend. Independent of Shanti and I and our journey into Mexico, Dr. Clark also ventured into Mexico and went through a similar experience with Salvador. He later wrote a description of what happened titled, "'Bad Trips' May Be The Best Trips." (A copy of his article can be found online).

I was, at the time, a 33-year-old theology student, parish minister, and university lecturer. Though I had begun the reading a photocopy of the Course (the Criswell edition), I had yet to understand the Course. Something is needed to reawaken the mind, so we can see our way out of our self-made prison—the "place" in which we seem to be "locked." Once the ego gets a hold on the mind, it *seems* like the door is locked and the key hidden. One's body may be in prison but the door to Heaven is never locked because it lies within one's mind. The body could be imprisoned and the mind totally free. It is we who shut ourselves out of Heaven by creating another world.

What is natural is Spirit. What is natural gives Life and Life cannot be limited to a body which is doomed to die. If you have trouble accepting this, then take the first step and realize that "society"—all of society or what we call "civilization"—is made up of egos, and the ego is unnatural. As the Course expresses it:

> *The light of truth is in us, where it was placed by God.*
> *It is the body that is outside us, and is not our concern.*
> *To be without a body is to be in our natural state.*
> *To recognize the light of truth in us*
> *is to recognize ourselves as we are.*

W-72.9:1–4

During my experience my ordinary ego-reality was rendered nonexistent, not because it was bad, but simply because my identity as Jon Mundy was unreal or meaningless. Faced with the exclusion of this ordinary ego-reality, I had an opportunity to look into a greater One. The event gave me an opportunity to understand who I am, free of the little self I created.

> *The self you made is not the Son of God.*
> *Therefore, this self does not exist at all.*
> *And anything it seems to do and think means nothing.*
> *It is neither bad nor good.*
> *It is unreal, and nothing more than that.*
>
> W–93. 5:1–5

ILLUMINATION

In a later experience in 1977, I felt as though I was illuminated—pure, utterly beautiful white light, luminous, perfectly tranquil, flowing with energy and wonder—what Heaven is when we just let go and let it happen. Never had I known a feeling like this—yet, I always have known it. I was ecstatically happy and filled with a sense of peace, contentment and well-being. Many things were clear. All of the issues and events around which anyone might experience pain were gone. I knew that I was forgiven because nothing needs to be forgiven. There is nothing to do but love, letting others be, guiding as much as possible without hurting myself or anyone.

This enlightenment lasted until the point of an encounter with a woman who had gone through a similar experience. I was open and it seemed total love until during the next day's processing with Salvador, she verbally attacked me. I don't remember what the attack was about. It doesn't matter. When the attack happened, it was as though a tiny nucleus, or little ball someplace within, defended itself. I was so peaceful, I said nothing. It all happened within the mind; the second the shift occurred, I began to lose it. How easily I gave eternity away. The ego's shell began to return. It did not return quickly, however, as I was just too open.

> *While you practice in this way,*
> *you leave behind everything that you now believe,*
> *and all the thoughts that you have made up.*
> *Properly speaking, this is the release from hell.*
> *Yet perceived through the ego's eyes,*
> *it is loss of identity and a descent into hell.*

W-44.5:4–5

> *If you can stand aside from the ego by ever so little,*
> *you will have no difficulty in recognizing*
> *that its opposition and its fears are meaningless.*

W-44.6:1

FEAR AND THE DESCENT INTO HELL

My experience was hellish. Hell is the fear of losing one's identity; and yet, this is an identity which must disappear. It is a shell which must be broken, a mask which must be removed in order for the soul to regain its vivacity.

> *What never was, can never be*
> *and there is no sacrifice in the letting go of a fantasy.*

Only by letting go of one's own little, ego-projected fantasy kingdom is it possible to have a glimpse into magnificence. Freedom from illusions lies simply in not believing them. How simple is the obvious.

The Guide Who brought you here remains with you,
and when you raise your eyes you will be ready
to look on terror with no fear at all.

T-19.IV.D.8:6

THERE IS NO FAITH IN FEAR

My fear came from the thought of the loss of the ego. I now know that there is nothing to be afraid of. What appears to be a loss is always a gain. We have the power not only to choose how we see the world, we have the power to choose how we see the universe.

Fear not that you will be abruptly lifted up and hurled into reality.
Time is kind, and if you use it on behalf of reality,
it will keep gentle pace with you in your transition.

T-16. VI. 8:1–2

The path of the Course is gentle and slow
otherwise the fear would be too great.

DR. KENNETH WAPNICK

Although I felt fear and expressed anger, I can imagine that another soul (able to release itself more freely than I) would have found the experience absolutely blissful. Indeed, my later experiences with Salvador were blissful. Fear is the one emotion we created. We could not have created it had we not felt guilty. God being love knows nothing of guilt or fear. There is no hell. There is no devil. There is no outside.

My life since has been an effort to find out more about that world beyond form, so that when I leave this body forever, I can more readily and freely step into Eternity.

Thus, the Holy Spirit operates within this temporal framework
even though He knows that time and space are not real.
However, He does not obliterate the belief in time and space,
which would awaken us from the dream too rapidly,
precipitating panic.

DR. KENNETH WAPNICK,
THE VAST ILLUSION: TIME ACCORDING TO A COURSE IN MIRACLES

The use of psychedelics is a bit like using dynamite to break through the doors of Heaven. I had awakened abruptly. I awoke from the dream of bodily form too quickly—in a panic. I *had* been hurled into reality, and I didn't know how to handle it. I needed to come back to "ordinary consciousness" even though I knew it meant being so very much less aware. Things are comprehensible in this world because they *seem to happen* sequentially.

Can you imagine what a state of mind without illusions is?
How it would feel?
Try to remember when there was a time,—perhaps a minute,
maybe even less—when nothing came to interrupt your peace;
when you were certain you were loved and safe.

Then try to picture what it would be like
to have that moment be extended
to the end of time and to eternity.
Then let the sense of quiet that you felt
be multiplied a hundred times,
and then be multiplied another hundred more.
And now you have a hint,
not more than just the faintest intimation
of the state your mind will rest in when the truth has come.

W-P.I.107.2:1–5 & 3:1

TIME STOPPED

One of the most interesting aspects of this vision is the sense of having seen it all before. If there is something that is eternal, and this life experience is temporal, then *seeing* can be understood as returning Home again—what I understand as *eternal return*, or what my friend P.M.H. Atwater calls *Future Memory*.

> *Such is each life; a seeming interval*
> *from birth to death and on to life again,*
> ***a repetition of an instant gone by***
> *long ago that cannot be relived.*
> *And all of time is but the mad belief*
> *that what is over is still here and now.*

T-26.V.13:3–4

Here are two descriptions of others who have had similar experiences with Ketamine:

I got deeper and deeper into this state, until at one point the world disappeared. I was no longer in my body. I didn't have a body. I reached a point at which I knew I was going to die. There was no question about it, no maybe I will, or "perhaps I will."

Then I reached a point at which I felt ready to die. It wasn't a question of choice, it was just a wave that carried me higher and higher, at the same time that I was having what in my normal state I would call the horror of death. It became obvious to me that it is not at all what I anticipated death to be. Except, I knew it was death, that something was dying.

I reached a point at which I gave it all away. I just yielded, and then I entered a space in which there weren't any words. The words have been used a thousand times—starting with "Buddha," "are at-one-with-the-universe," "recognizing your godhead"—all those words. I later used to explore what I have experienced. The feeling was that I'm "home." I didn't want to go anywhere, and I didn't need to go anywhere. It was a bliss state of a kind I never experienced before."

PETER STAFFORD, *PSYCHEDELICS ENCYCLOPEDIA*,

1992, PAGES 393, 394

Much of this previous experience has about it qualities of what the Course refers to as a Holy Instant. Here is another experience:

One should be lying down, because they will be unconscious of their body shortly after. As the high is coming on, there is a break in the continuity of consciousness. Soon after this point I found myself in a swirling psychedelic universe. Frequently, there was no recollection of ever having been myself, been born, having a personality or body, or even knowing of planet earth.

The experience was one of being in total orgasm with the universe. I felt like I was in hyperspace, simultaneously connected to all things. Billions of images and perception were simultaneously flowing though my circuits. I was not bound into three dimensions. I experienced backward and forward in time as well with the current moment being the center of intensity.

I felt as though there had been a major and permanent shift in the "fabric of reality." Sometimes I felt like a single atom or point of consciousness adrift in a swirling vortex of energies, like a single cell within a being of galactic proportion. The experience was of titanic proportion in the merging of energy, intent, and awareness, yet lucidity articulated to the minutest spiraling details. All the while I felt very relaxed and at home in this universe. Even though any support of reality, identity, or stability were dissolved at the speed of light, I did not experience any fear, as if the one who would experience fear at losing these things was not a part of me.

As the waves of experience passed through me, I felt a bit like a kid on a roller coaster. Although he's about to have an exhilarating experience while going over a hill, deeper in his mind he's confident that the roller coaster will stay on its tracks. The experience was so otherworldly that a normal mind can't even conceive of experiencing in this manner.

D.M. TURNER, *THE ESSENTIAL PSYCHEDELIC GUIDE*, 1994, PAGES 64–66.

Shanti had a totally different experience. Apparently, she was able to let go and simply disappear. As she entered her experience, she no doubt took the roller coaster ride. She kept saying, "Wow!" and "Oh my God!" and "Look at that!" She was more accepting of death than I.

This experience occurred in July and as I was not teaching that summer, I returned from Mexico to spend the month of August and early September living in a log cabin a mile back in the woods near Cold Spring, in Putnam County, New York. There I typed up this description from the notes I made in Mexico. There too, I was able to observe the fabric of nature as never before. There was an exciting new way of experiencing, seeing, knowing, and connecting with everything. All of my relationships became more immediate. I was more interested in just being with people—in getting close to them and knowing what was going on with them. Speaking about my own interests seemed inconsequential.

In a similar way, Anita Moorjani said that after her experience, "I felt a bond with everyone in a way I had never before—not only all the members of my family, but every nurse, doctor who came into my room. I had an outpouring of love for each person who came to do something for me." I'll have this experience of connectedness again in 2001 when I accepted the fact that I might be dying from cancer and again in 2007 as I was coming out of a coma from encephalitis.

THE INSANITY WE CALL REALITY

After the experience, it was as though I was peacefully looking down on life not in condemnation (as the ego would do), rather in blessing of Life. I was able to see without being caught in the middle of whatever dynamic unfolded in front of me. It was possible to pass over much of the game-playing and move more quickly into meaningful contact. As the days and weeks went by, however, I could feel the socialization process around me, pulling me back to what I was before. I had, however, obtained enough objectivity that I could not be pulled all the way back into the insanity we call reality.

One morning I woke up at dawn and went out on the cabin deck to breath in the fresh morning air. Looking off to the left of the deck, I saw a Great Horned Owl sitting on a path—just sitting there on the ground. I went down the path and slowly walked straight up to this mighty bird. I got closer and closer. I stopped—standing only about fifteen feet from the owl. He did not move. He just looked at me—watchfully—blinked his velvet eyes a few times and continued staring at me. His huge yellow gaze went deep inside. We continued to stare at each other for a long time. The phone rang. I was expecting a call, and I ran back into the cabin. Afterward, when I went back out onto the deck, he was gone. Later, I attended a conference in Montreal Canada where I listening to an native American talking about the importance of Animal Totems. After, I told him about my experience with the owl, he said that the owl was there to help implant in my mind the memory of what I had learned in my journey.

As I now read more deeply into the Course, suddenly so much of it made sense. I understood what it meant when it said there is no time, no world, no body and no "me" in the ordinary sense of the word. I began on that cabin deck *A Course in Miracles* study groups and I threw myself into a study of near-death experience. I became a voracious reader of anything I could find on the new physics, or what is sometimes called "psycho-physics." These works offered amazing insight into what had happened. I got excited by reading Dr. Fritjof Capra's *The Tao of Physics*. I made contact with Capra and offered to put together a workshop for him in New York City. Edie had a large living room in her brownstone and volunteered the space for the workshop. It was perfect and it was packed.

I also did further work with Dr. Stanislav (Stan) Grof, who began his research in psychedelics in his native Czechoslovakia in 1956, and I sponsored workshops with Stan in New York City. In May 1978, he came to stay with me at High Rock while he also lectured at Wainwright House in Rye, New York. And, I sponsored a Conference on Psycho-Physics for the Academy of Religion and Psychical Research at Union Theological Seminary in New York City.

In 1978, I sponsored a weekend workshop at High Rock Spring with Itzhak Bentov (1923–1979). Itzhak was a Czech-born, Israeli American scientist, inventor, mystic, and author. He invented several medical devices, including one that kept the heart in rhythm during operations and the steerable cardiac catheter that transformed cardiac surgery. Itzhak was a very soft-spoken, deeply spiritual man. His primary work was on the study of brain frequencies. I had become excited by reading his book, *Stalking the Wild Pendulum*, a terrific book on the nature of reality. When I told Itzhak about my *Holy Hell* experience, he laughed and said something about my accidentally stepping into the bardo. His wife was there, and she laughed too, as he told her about my experience. She seemed to know what he was talking about.

In Buddhism the bardo is an intermediate, transitional state of existence after life on Earth. The bardo is explained in the *Tibetan Book of the Dead*, first composed during the eighth century. The book was lost for several centuries. Then, similar to the *Dead Sea Scrolls* (discovered in segments between 1946 and 1956), the *Tibetan Book of the Dead* was rediscovered in the fourteenth century. According to the Tibetan tradition, after death when one's consciousness is not connected with a physical body, one can experience a variety of phenomena, including the clearest possible experiences of reality. For the prepared and appropriately trained individual, the bardo offers a state of opportunity for liberation, since transcendental insight can arise from the experience. For the untrained, it offers the opportunity for a rapid development in awareness.

Itzhak was killed on May 25, 1979, as a passenger on American Airlines, Flight 191 that crashed at O'Hare International in Chicago. Moments after takeoff, an engine detached, tearing the plane apart. The crash killed all 271 people onboard and two on the ground—the deadliest plane crash on United States soil to-date. Although I don't know how this could have happened, his wife later said that he contacted her after his passing and told her that he had seen what was going to happen as he boarded the plane. He went ahead and boarded anyway because he knew he would be needed as a guide for the other passengers in their transition.

SECTION III

Life and the Body

SEVEN

Let There Be Life

There is no life outside of Heaven.
Where God created life, there life must be.
In any state apart from Heaven life is illusion.

At best it seems like life; at worst, like death.
Yet both are judgments on what is not life,
equal in their inaccuracy and lack of meaning.

Life not in Heaven is impossible,
and what is not in Heaven is not anywhere.

Outside of Heaven, only the conflict of illusion stands;
senseless, impossible and beyond all reason,
and yet perceived as an eternal barrier to Heaven.

Illusions are but forms. Their content is never true.

T-23.II.19:2–9

My friend Ed Spath, MD, who left this world in January of 2015, told me a story of how he had saved a young girl from drowning one summer day on a beach when he was still a young doctor. As he pulled the girl out of the water, she was lifeless. Holding her upside down to get the water out of her, he said he suddenly felt *life* return to her lifeless body. Webster's dictionary defines "life" as: (1) the condition that distinguishes organic from inorganic objects and (2) the period of animate existence of an individual organism.

BEHOLD THE PLANET OF THE TARDIGRADES

If the following sounds like science fiction, check it out online. Tardigrades (or water bears) are water-dwelling micro-animals, so small they can be seen only under a microscope. They have eight legs, each with four to eight claws, and a menacing-looking telescopic mouth with clawlike teeth that can reach out and grab its prey—big things like bacteria.

This earth could be said to be the planet of the tardigrades, as they have been here for about 500 million years. On a historic timeline, we humans just arrived here a few minutes ago. Just like ants, tardigrades have survived each of the five major periods of extinction of life on earth, and just like the ants there are many billions more of them than there are humans on this planet. Tardigrades can withstand temperatures from just above absolute zero to well above the boiling point of water; pressures six times greater than those found in the deepest ocean trenches; and ionizing radiation at doses hundreds of times higher than the lethal dose for a human; and they can live in the vacuum of outer space. They can *live* for ten years or more without food or water.

> *I am come that you might have life*
> *and that you might have it more abundantly.*
>
> JOHN 10:10

The existence of tardigrades raises questions about the dictionary definition of life as *a period of animate existence of an organism*. We may need to expand on our dictionary definition of life. Although they are *animals*, tardigrades can exist so long in a dormant state that they are *almost* more like seeds. Are seeds alive, or do they just have the *potential* for life? Maybe we too are not yet fully alive. Maybe we simply have the potential for Life. The reports of

near-death experiences tell us that there is a Life so far beyond what
we call "life" that this life is really dreaming.

You have chosen a sleep in which you have had bad dreams,
but the sleep is not real and God calls you to awake.

T-6.IV.6:3

Thought cannot be made into flesh
except by belief, since thought is not physical.
Yet thought is communication,
for which the body can be used.
This is the only natural use to which it can be put.
To use the body unnaturally
is to lose sight of the Holy Spirit's purpose,
and thus to confuse the goal of His curriculum.

T-8.VII.7:4–7

LIFE IS THOUGHT

What if *life* is not something that requires the presence of carbon
and oxygen? Does God breathe oxygen? Is God dependent upon anything? What if *Life* has nothing to do with space and time or form
as we understand it? Life, Mind, and Spirit are synonymous and are
incorporeal—nonmaterial. *Life is thought* (W-54.2:3), and thought
does not have a form. According to cosmology, the only thing that
can go faster than the speed of light would have to be something
that does not have mass. What does not have mass? Thought does
not have mass. The mind does not have mass. Love does not have
mass. Spirit does not have mass.

The miracle of life is ageless,
born in time but nourished in eternity.

T-19.IV.C.10:6

Everything is accomplished through life,
and life is of the mind and in the mind.
The body neither lives nor dies,
because it cannot contain you who are life.

T-6.V.A.1:3–4

A body is not what gives us Life. Neither does a body die, because no "body" lives. The body is a tiny, mad idea that has never left its source in the mind. While the mind cannot attack, it can make fantasies and direct the body to act them out. Death, were it possible, would be the final and complete disruption of communication between ourselves and God.

Those who fear death see not how often and how loudly
they call to it, and bid it come to save them from communication.
For death is seen as safety, the great dark savior from the light of
truth, the answer to the Answer,
the silencer of the Voice that speaks for God.

T-19.IV.C.7:1–2

THE EGO AND THE HOLY SPIRIT

The body is the ego's chosen home. The ego is dedicated to death, not knowing that Life in God is the only Life there is. There is no Eternity in any body. Stars are born and stars die. It takes millions or even many billions of years for them to complete their life/death cycle, but all "things" die. Thus, there is no Eternity in any "thing."

In Judaism, the Holy Spirit is called *Ruach* (Breath) *Hakodesh* (Holy). The word "Spirit," from the Latin *spirare*, means "blowing," "wind," "breath," and "air." Closely associated with wind and breath is *voice*. The Holy Spirit is the "Voice," or, if you will, *the thought of God* quietly directing us very specifically, if we are willing to follow direction.

OUR AGATHOKAKOLOGICAL MINDS

I have a subscription to *Merriam-Webster's* Word of the Day. Each morning, a new vocabulary word appears in my email. Sometimes it's a fun word like "bumfuzzled," meaning "confused," or "flapdoodle," meaning "nonsense." Or the word may be one you can use to win at Scrabble. Sometimes, just for fun, the word will be a jaw-breaking, oversized word.

One such oversized word is "agathokakological" (that's ag-a-tho-kak-o-log-i-cal). It's seventeen letters long and means having a split or divided mind; a mixed mind—good and bad—as in the song lyrics "I love you. I hate you." It is made up of the Greek root *agath* (good), *kako* (as in *cac*, meaning, well, you know—nasty), and *logical*, the adjectival suffix based on *logos*, meaning "word." We all have *agathokakological* minds. We all have split personalities. We all experience the coexistence of contradictory thoughts. The Course describes this as right- and wrong-mindedness.

TWO USES OF MIND

There are two uses of the word "mind" in the Course. Capital "M" Mind, or the Mind of God, is the equivalent of Spirit, Love, Heaven, Truth, Eternity, and Freedom. This is "the Mind" of which we are all a part—the Mind in which there are no separated parts and degrees. We only "think" that we can "think" a thought outside the Mind of

God. Trying to think a thought outside the Mind of God leads to the dreaming of the world.

Lowercase "m" mind refers to the ego, the agent of choice in this dreamworld of changing form and separation. We all have minds; we are free to believe what we want. We can align our minds with capital "M" Mind and, thus, with the Holy Spirit (the Voice for God in our minds) or with the lowercase "m" mind, the ego (also referred to in the Course as wrong-mindedness or the insane mind). Mind—the Mind of God—is the fundamental foundation of all existence. Everything is in and of the Mind of God.

Man can try to name love, showering upon it all the
names at his command,
and still he will involve himself in endless self-deceptions.
If he possesses a grain of wisdom, he will lay down his arms
and name the unknown by the more unknown . . .
by the name of God.

DR. CARL JUNG (1875–1961), SWISS PSYCHIATRIST

THE MIND

We all have minds. Animals have minds. Even plants have an inner sense. Though it has no eyes, a vine knows which direction it should reach out to in order to get hold of a branch. Ultimately, it's all mind. Only the mind is real. Only the mind is capable of illumination. Only the Mind can "know." We come to Heaven through *revelation*, through *remembering* or through *re-cognition* that we are already Home.

But seek you first the kingdom of God,
and his righteousness;
and all these things shall be added to you.

MATTHEW 6:33

The Mind has the power to choose between Heaven and earth, between the ego and Spirit, between time and Eternity. To talk about the power of the Mind does not mean using the power of the Mind to get things in the world. If we're following God's Plan for Salvation, we will find our way Home. We'll even find Home when we do not actively pursue it. In the school of hard knocks, however, the tuition is quite high, and it is much more fun to live a guided life than to live one that is ego-driven.

Like ice turning into liquid, which turns into steam, the awakening mind gets lighter and lighter as we melt back into Spirit. The Holy Spirit is in us in a literal sense—in the mind with which we think, acting as "the communication link" between ourselves and God. The Holy Spirit bridges the gap between our sleeping minds and the Awakened Mind of God. He reminds us of our True Identity as that which is part of and not separate from God.

The word for *mind* in German is *Geist*.
The word for *spirit* in German is *Geist*.
The word for *mind* in French is *Esprit*.
The word for *spirit* in French is *Esprit*.
The word for *mind* in Dutch is *Geest*.
The word for *spirit* in Dutch is *Geest*.

Mind is invisible—it has no form. Spirit is invisible—it has no form. Love is invisible—it has no form. God is invisible. God has no form. We refer to God and the Holy Spirit as "he" because we are so prone to thinking in terms of form that it is hard to think of God without a body. In some near-death experiences, especially those of children, God is *seen* or experienced as a grandfatherly being, as it was in the case of Helen Schucman's mystical experience in the subway in New York City. God is seen that way, as it is an easy first-step adjustment that can be made.

Spirit gives life and flesh counts for nothing.

JOHN 6:63

GOD IS LIFE

British actor Richard Mansfield's last words were, "God is Love." And his wife responded, "God is Life." Every religion defines God as Love. God is also Mind and Life. *Life* comes as a preface to (ante-dates) the body. Life does not begin with the birth of a body; nor does it end with the death of a body. If God is Life and God is Love, then Love is Life and Life is Love. Therefore, the more alive we are, the more in love we are, and the more in love we are, the more alive we are. So it is that we have Eternal Life!

There is no question but one you should ever ask of yourself;
*Do I want **to know** my Father's Will for me?*

T-8.VI.8:1

Do we really want to know what God's Will is for us? Do we want to know it so much that we are willing to become God's Will? It is possible to know God's Will. Jesus did it. All of those we call enlightened beings have done it. I think Bill Thetford did it. I think Ken Wapnick did it, and anyone can do it because it is already true. It is possible to know and do God's Will perfectly as we remove the blocks to an awareness of Love's presence. Begin with Love and see what comes forth out of Love. *To know* is *to do*—to make real, *to bring to Life.*

There is no work to do in Heaven because creation is play.

As your function in Heaven is creation,
so your function on earth is healing.

T-12.VII.4:7

Our function in Heaven is creation, that is, *the extension of Love.* This is the function of God and of ourselves. Our function in this world is healing. Healing is the miracle that occurs when we accept responsibility and forgiveness ourselves.

We don't have to get rid of the body in order to know Eternity. That will happen soon enough and in its own time. As Heaven is in the Mind, all we have to do is to awaken to the magnificence that is already ours. We have seen that words like "God," "Life," "Heaven," "Truth," and "Love" are synonyms. Just as life and death are incompatible and irreconcilable, God and the ego are incompatible and irreconcilable. Either there is life or there is death. God is Life and an opposite to Life cannot exist. Likewise, an opposite to God does not exist; therefore, there is in reality no ego. Egos exist only as fantasies, and fantasies are always lifeless.

Life has no opposite, for it is God.
Life and death seem to be opposites
because you have decided death ends life.
Forgive the world, and you will understand that
everything that God created cannot have an end,
and nothing He did not create is real.

M-20.5:5–7

To forgive the world means to give up any hard-heartedness we may have against anyone on this earth. Remember, we are all equals. If we think anyone is of greater or lesser value than ourselves, we close the door to Heaven on ourselves. With even greater ease, we could open that door. Those who report near-death experiences often report that what they experience is truly life more abundantly. Dale Black, in his book, *Flight to Heaven*, writes:

> Vibrant life permeated everything.
> All these [beings] weren't just around me, they were inside me.
> And it was wonderful, more wonderful than anything I had experienced.
> I felt as if I belonged there. I didn't want to leave ever.

THE MISSION—LIVING LIFE FEARLESSLY

Those who come back from near-death experiences come back because they feel they have some mission to fulfill. Heaven is always described as so wonderful you just don't want to leave. When most folks have a near-death experience, they let go completely and willingly. In Anita Moorjani's case, she said she could feel both her father and her friend Soni telling her, and, as she writes in *Dying To Be Me*, "Now that you know the truth of who you really are, go back and live your life fearlessly!" I read of another near-death experience in which that individual was also told to go back and live *fearlessly!* I was watching a show on *Doomsday Preppers*—folks who are preparing for the end of the world by stockpiling food and ammunition—and realized it was all about fear. It was all about the preservation of the body even to the point of killing other bodies who might want some of your stash of food.

Waken from time,
and answer fearlessly the Call of Him
Who gave eternity to you in your creation.
On this side of the bridge to timelessness you understand nothing.
But as you step lightly across it, upheld "by" timelessness,
you are directed straight to the Heart of God.
At its center, and only there, you are safe forever,
because you are complete forever.
There is no veil the Love of God in us together cannot lift.
The way to truth is open.
Follow it with me.

T-16.IV.13:5–11

As we give up on living out of fear and live life valiantly and confidently in each encounter, then it does not matter what the externals of life may be. Then we can live fully and fearlessly in the face of whatever this life throws our way. Tell me you don't know what you are supposed to do with your life and I'll say you're in denial. Everyone knows. Our job is to be Love, and in that Love there is healing and wholeness and the remembrance of Eternity.

Nothing exists outside of the Mind of God. God is neither male nor female. God is One and cannot be divided. We can oppose God but we can't help being God. God knows you as his Only Child. There is then only One Child, One Innocent Mind within the Heart of God. Eternity transcends physicality. The word "disciple" (*sannyasin*) in Sanskrit means "colorless" or "transparent." There are no Christians, Muslims, Buddhists, Hindus, or Jews in Heaven. All religions are, at best, learning devices—tools that may help to get us Home.

What you have made invisible is the only truth,
and what you have not heard is the only Answer.

T-12.VIII.4:4

What we have made invisible is Love itself—the most beautiful thing of all. The only truth is Love. Love is invisible though it can be demonstrated in many forms. Deep inside we know God, but we block awareness of God's presence. The mind is *naturally* abstract. The ego is specific and concrete.

> *The ego has built a shabby and unsheltering home for you,*
> *because it cannot build otherwise.*
> *Do not try to make this impoverished house stand.*
> *Its weakness is your strength.*
> *Only God could make a home that is worthy of His creations,*
> *who have chosen to leave it empty by their own dispossession.*

> *Yet His home will stand forever,*
> *and is ready for you when you choose to enter it.*

T-4.I.11:1–6

The ego is nothing disguised as something. It is the part of the mind that loves being on its own—though it is also lonely. It is a wrong-minded attempt to perceive ourselves as we wish to be, rather than as we are. It is a separated self, "made" as a substitute for the Self that God created. It is a part of the mind that believes existence is defined by separation.

> *The ego's fundamental wish is to replace God.*
> *In fact, the ego is the physical embodiment of that wish.*
> *For it is that wish that seems to surround the mind with a body.*

W-72.2:1–3

The ego is the mind's belief that it is completely on its own. It is the "belief" that it is possible to live outside or "free of" the Mind of

God. The ego is understood only by transcending it, at which point we have no use for it.

> *You look for permanence in the impermanent, for love where*
> *there is none, for safety in the midst of danger;*
> *immortality within the darkness of the dream of death.*
> *Who could succeed where contradiction is the setting of his*
> *searching, and the place to which he comes to find stability?*
>
> W-131.1:2–3

The ego begs us not to listen to the Holy Spirit, for if we do, we will be annihilated. Indeed, the ego will be annihilated, but then how can you destroy a fantasy? All we can do is to awaken from a dream of death, remember who we are, and come Home to God.

> *I do not attack your ego.*
> *I do work with your higher mind,*
> *the home of the Holy Spirit, whether you are asleep or awake,*
> *just as your ego does with your lower mind, which is its home.*
> *Christ is in me, and where He is God must be,*
> *for Christ is part of Him.*
>
> T-4.VI.11:1–2

THE CHRIST MIND

You are the Christ, the Self, the Son of God or the Daughter of God, if you prefer. God does not see separation. He sees no difference among his children. Here, traditional Christians and the Course go down different roads. In traditional Christianity, Jesus is the only Son of God. Jesus in the Course says:

"No man cometh unto the Father but by me"
does not mean that I am in any way separate or different
from you except in time, and time does not really exist.
The statement is more meaningful in terms of a vertical
rather than a horizontal axis.
You stand below me and I stand below God.

T-1.III.4:1–3

Christ *is* the Universal Mind of God in which we are all One. We are all the Christ. There is only One Mind, only One Will, only One Christ. The Christ Mind is innocent. It cannot condemn. It can only bless. The Holy Spirit is the Christ Mind—aware of Knowledge that lies beyond perception. There is no Will other than God's Will, and the Christ Mind follows only God's Will. We cannot be separate from the Mind of God, and deep down inside, everyone knows this is true. Thus, Jesus asks us to say to ourselves:

If you hope to spare yourself from fear
there are some things you must realize, and realize fully.
The mind is very powerful, and never loses its creative force.
It never sleeps. Every instant it is creating.

T-2.VI.9:4–7

When your body and your ego and your dreams are gone,
you will know that you will last forever.
Perhaps you think this is accomplished through death,
but nothing is accomplished through death,
because death is nothing.

T-6.V.A.1:1–2

EIGHT

Relinquishing Our Dedication to Death

And the Lord God commanded the man, saying,
Of every tree of the garden you may freely eat:
But of the tree of the knowledge of good and evil,
you shall not eat of it:
for in the day you eat thereof you shall surely die.

GENESIS 2:16–17

To you and your brother,
in whose special relationship the Holy Spirit entered,
it is given to release and be released
from the dedication to death.

T-19.IV.C.1:1

According to biblical scholars, there is more than one stream of thought and, therefore, more than one author writing in the book of Genesis. There are, for example, two creation stories: one in Genesis 1:1–2:3 and a second in Genesis 2:4 through the end of Genesis 3. According to the second of these narratives, because Adam and Eve ate of the fruit of the tree of the knowledge of good and evil—something they had been forbidden to do—God cursed them and condemned them to death.

Into eternity, where all is one, there crept a tiny, mad idea,
at which the Son of God remembered not to laugh.

T-27.VIII.6:2

SEPARATION, OR THE DETOUR INTO FEAR

Only a "separated mind" can think it possible to exist outside of God's protection and Love. The ego and the Holy Spirit know nothing of each other because the Holy Spirit cannot recognize something that does not exist. There are no egos in Heaven, and Heaven is our only reality.

The Adam and Eve story tells the tale very well.
The birth of the ego was the creation of hell.

The birth of the ego was the creation of hell, as the belief in hell is unavoidable to those who identify with the ego. The good news is this: the memory of God is always possible, and then, in the memory of God, there is no ego and there is no hell. Although the ego has no reality, it *appears* as though a separation has occurred; after all, we do all have split (divided) minds. Eternity is consistent. A split mind is inconsistent. This *seeming separation* is referred to in the Course as "the dreaming of the world." And the body is the central figure in this dreaming.

Heaven remains your one alternative to this strange world you
made and all its ways; its shifting patterns and uncertain goals,
its painful pleasures and its tragic joys.
God made no contradictions.
What denies its own existence and attacks itself is not of Him.
He did not make two minds, with Heaven as the

glad effect of one,
and earth the other's sorry outcome
which is Heaven's opposite in every way.

W-131.7:1–4

There can be no separation in Heaven. Separation from God is actually impossible. This *seeming reality* is what we call the world. As strange as it sounds, at no time is this world real. Heaven is reality. That is why when people have near-death experiences and they get a little "peek" into Eternity, they come back and say that *that is reality*; that is Home, and this world is a dream. Not only is the world not real, but the body also is not real, precisely because it is impermanent. For this reason, the death of the body can be thought of as an awakening to reality rather than a loss of reality, or an awakening into truth rather than a loss of truth.

Heaven is the home of perfect purity,
and God created it for you.

T-22.II.13:6

The Course represents a radical monism. All there is that is really real is God, Love, Truth, Reality, Eternity, Heaven—really Big words. Just for a moment, a character, whom for fun we might call *Umeuswe* (that's *you* and *me* and *us* and *we*), decided it was possible to think a thought outside of the Mind of God. That *tiny, mad idea* gave rise to this whole world and every aspect of it.

Your mind is one with God's.
Denying this and thinking otherwise has held your ego together,
but has literally split your mind.

T-4.IV.2:7

Before this split came into the mind, there was just pure, simple thinking, as exists within the minds of animals. Mark Bekoff, PhD, in his book *Minding Animals*, says that some animals have a sense of self, as in "this is my tail," "this is my territory," or "this is my mate." Only a few animals, however, such as the great apes and dolphins, can pass the mirror test, where they recognize themselves in a mirror. No animal, however, is capable of "self-reflective thought." That is, while animals think, so far as we know, *they do not think about thinking*. Animals—indeed, all of nature—knows God without knowing that they know.

CONSCIOUSNESS AND AWARENESS, PERCEPTION AND KNOWLEDGE

One of the main characteristics of mystical and near-death experiences is *the oceanic sense* of blending, merging, or becoming one with nature or music or perhaps the beloved. In Emily Brontë's *Wuthering Heights*, the heroine, Catherine, cries out, "I am Heathcliff." Anita Moorjani said that she did not just speak with her father; "she became him."

Consciousness implies subject-object and the awareness of an outside. There is a perceiver and a perceived. An ant moves its *feelers* around to *feel* what is in front of it. Thus, it has consciousness *of* something. Consciousness occurs on the level of perception. The Course distinguishes between *perception* and *knowledge*. *Consciousness*, being *the first split introduced into the mind after the separation*, made the mind a perceiver rather than a creator (T-3.IV.2:1).

Knowledge is Heaven, the awareness of God and his unified creation in which there is no difference. Knowledge of Heaven is, thus, exclusive of the world of perception. It is not as though one is *seeing* something in the subject-object sense; rather, one simply experiences unity without duality.

Because of your likeness to your Creator you are creative.
No child of God can lose this ability because it is inherent
in what he is, but he can use it inappropriately by projecting.

T-2.I.1:5

The setup in the creation story sounds like one of those experiments where a psychologist puts a bowl of M&M's® on a table in front of a child and then tells the child that he is going to leave the room for a few minutes and the child is not to eat any of the candy while he is gone. Of course, the temptation to eat the forbidden candy is great, and who is going to notice if a few M&M's go missing?

Adam's "sin" could have touched no one,
had he not believed it was the Father
Who drove him out of Paradise.
For in that belief the knowledge of the Father [Heaven] was lost,
since only those who do not understand Him could believe it.

T-13.IN.3:6–7

WHAT IS DEATH?

According to the second creation story in Genesis, God punishes Adam and Eve and, therefore, all of humankind by giving us death as a consequence of our disobedience. Does the cessation of bodily existence end everything? Is Adam's *sin* our sin? Are we cursed because of what Adam did? Or is the birth of "self-consciousness" (awareness of a separate bodily self) merely a temporal loss of the awareness of our Home in God?

For what the seeing look upon "is" sinless.
No one who loves can judge,

> *and what he sees is free of condemnation.*
>
> T-20.VII.9:6–7

> *God does not believe in retribution.*
> *His Mind does not create that way.*
>
> T-3.I.3:4–5

FREEDOM FROM CONDEMNATION

The ego's version of justice is that sin is not error but a reality, which calls for vengeance. Sinners must, therefore, be punished. I once heard a televangelist say, "There must be a hell and sinners must go there; otherwise, it just wouldn't be fair." God does not believe in reprisal, and he takes no revenge. With the onset of the experience of a divided mind ("knowledge of good and evil"), our minds now *seem* directed by an alien ego, which exists in opposition to God.

> *The Bible says that a deep sleep fell upon Adam,*
> *and nowhere is there reference to his waking up.*
>
> T-2.I.3:6

GOD DOES NOT HAVE AN EGO

We have not hurt God. We have not sinned; rather, we have been much mistaken. We have fallen asleep and we are having some disturbing dreams. Like Alice down the rabbit hole, we are in a strange world in which things *are* turned upside down. Our sense is that something is wrong but we don't know what it is; nor do we know how to fix it. In *reality*, nothing is wrong except that we see ourselves as separate from God. We cannot escape from what we are. You are spirit and forever a Child of God. In this direction does freedom lie.

There is almost always some problem in our dreams—we're lost and we can't find our way home, the car won't start, or we're driving the car with our eyes closed. There is some problem and it needs to be fixed. We need to find our way home, and we keep being thwarted in the process. Atul Gawande, MD, in his fine book, *Being Mortal*, describes a recurring dream in which he finds one of his patients in bed with him. He then dreams that he is trying to get the patient back into the hospital without arousing suspicion but he can never find the patient's room. This is a typical ego-anxiety dream. Many dreams are like this. Anxiety characterizes our day and nighttime dreams. We awaken from our nighttime dreams only to find we have a new, perhaps even more pressing set of problems: taxes to be paid, health issues, debt issues. Topping the list are all of our many special relationships.

God is not angry or upset with us because we push him out of our minds. God knows we will eventually turn around and come Home. We will, all in time, awaken from dreaming. The memory of Eternity resides in every mind and we have a communication link (the Holy Spirit) that bridges the gap between ourselves and God. We have, in fact, already awakened. It's a matter of our re-cognizing what we already know.

Opposition to God can only arise in a dualistic universe. In a nondualistic universe, there is no good *and* evil. There is no other. There is no outside. There is only Oneness. In a dualistic universe, we think that we can defeat God by not following his Will, but this only leads to unhappiness.

> *All real pleasure comes from doing God's Will.*
>
> T-1.VII.1:4.

> *There is no stone in all the ego's embattled citadel that*
> *is more heavily defended than the idea that sin is real.*
>
> T-19.II.7:1

THE REALITY OF SIN

The idea of sin is wholly sacrosanct to the ego's way of thinking. Indeed, sin is the most "holy" concept in the ego's thought system. How could God be mad at us because we are sleeping?

> *For the wages of sin "is" death, and how can the immortal die?*
>
> T-19.II.3:6

God did not drive us out of the Garden of Eden. We left Home of our own volition. In fact, we ran away. Having left Home, we have fallen into the dreaming of the world. Reality, God can only give. God, being Life, cannot take Life away. Only the body—an idol in the dream of separation—dies. God offers only mercy and Life more abundant.

> *The body is the ego's idol;*
> *the belief in sin made flesh and then projected outward.*
> *This produces what seems to be a wall of flesh around the mind,*
> *keeping it prisoner in a tiny spot of space and time,*
> *beholden unto death, and given but an instant in which*
> *to sigh and grieve and die in honor of its master.*
>
> T-20.VI.11:1–2

> *We see in the beginning only what we can see*
> *and we open our eyes slowly to eternity.*

EAT, DRINK, AND BE MERRY, FOR TOMORROW WE DIE

The body, the world, and time are all distractions and hiding places from God. I love it when I am reading the Course and I come across a line and exclaim, "What?!" Here is a "what" from the Course: "At

no single instant does the body exist at all" (T-18.VII.3:1). *What?!*
The body does not exist at all, simply because it is an ephemeral
dream-figure, which contains no lasting reality. Having said that,
we want to do the best we can with this ephemeral body. The body
is "a learning device," and as long as we seem to be proprietors of
a body, we can use this tool to help us find our way Home. We do
not demean the body, do away with the body, or deny its *seeming*
reality. Its past and future make it *seem real*, and therein lies the
illusion. The body serves a function in time. The body and time are
a means—not an end.

> *A body [ego] and mind [spirit] cannot both exist.*
> *Make no attempt to reconcile the two,*
> *for one denies the other can be real. . . .*
> *If you are spirit,*
> *then the body must be meaningless to your reality.*
>
> W-96.3:4–5, 7

> *The term "mind" is used to represent*
> *the activating agent of spirit, supplying its creative energy.*
>
> C-1.1:1

Mind is the activating agent of Spirit. Mind is also the agent's
choice. We have free will. It is one of the characteristics of our
divinity. The body can be *activated* only by the mind. Who rules
the body? One day soon (not very long from now), our bodies, the
physical being occupying space and time like other bodies, will disappear. If your body is cremated, turns to ashes, and is scattered to
the wind—where are you then?—certainly not in the ashes.

> *The ego regards the body as its home,*
> *and tries to satisfy itself through the body.*

> *But the idea that this is possible is a decision of the mind,*
> *which has become completely confused*
> *about what is really possible.*

T-4.II.7:8–9

THE BODY AND THE BELIEF IN DEATH

To make the body real is to make the underlying thought the body symbolizes real. It is not possible to exist outside of the Mind of God. We can, for a little while, hang out in space-time and pretend we know nothing of that figure called God. Again, this is what the Course calls "dreaming of the world." Separation from God can occur only in a fantasy, and fantasy is not reality.

> *What has the body really given you that justifies*
> *your strange belief that in it lies salvation?*
> *Do you not see that this is the belief in death?*

T-19.IV.B.2:4–5

What sacrifice is there in detaching from the body? None. What do we give up? Nothing. What do we lose? Nothing. How can something go missing that was never there? The Course is not asking us to give up on the world. It is not asking us to renounce pleasures. It is simply asking us to see that there is something much deeper going on. Spirit has something to say. We must be willing to listen. When we are willing to hide nothing, we are also entering into communion. Spirit is trying to awaken us to an awareness of Heaven—right here, right now.

> *Where can guilt be, when the belief in sin is gone?*
> *And where is death, when its great advocate*
> *is heard no more?*

T-19.IV.B.7:8–9

TIME IS A BOUNDARY

Einstein believed that the universe was eternal. Then along came Edwin Hubble. In 1922, he looked through the lens of the then newly installed hundred-inch Hooker telescope at Mount Wilson Observatory in California, and he discovered a limit called *time*. The universe has an age. It is, give or take a few hundred million years, about 14 billion years old. Age is a boundary. There is a beginning and an end. Our sun is about 5 billion years old, and about 5 billion years from now, it is destined to die. When the sun dies, everything on earth will, of course, also die. Just like the sun, our bodies are bound by time, and they are destined to die. There is a point of birth and a point of death. All bodies end, and when they do, they are either turned into ashes or returned to the earth as food for worms.

The ego defines "existence" as separation. To the Holy Spirit there can be no separation. The ego depends on the concrete, the material form, the outside. Einstein was correct in his belief that eternity is reality. It is the nontemporal, nonphysical Universal Love of God that is Eternal and, therefore, real. Eternity is not limited by physicality or temporality, because Eternal reality has no form.

Nothing so blinding as perception of form.
For sight of form means understanding has been obscured.

T-22.III.6:7–8

The outside world is a gigantic distraction. To the ego, it's what's on the *outside* that matters. The Kingdom of Heaven is inside; yet, we look outside for our definition of reality. What's inside is fact. What's outside is fiction.

> *What I'm looking for is not out there, it is in me.*
>
> HELEN KELLER (1880–1968)

God is not angry because we look outside. Looking outside for answers is dreaming. Dreaming only occurs when we are sleeping. We are unhappy insofar as we think dreaming is reality—knowing deep inside that dreaming is fiction. Reality reappears in awakening.

> *Only the mind can create because spirit has already been created,*
> *and the body is a learning device for the mind.*
> *Learning devices are not lessons in themselves.*
> *Their purpose is merely to facilitate learning.*
>
> T-2.IV.3:1–3

LEARNING DEVICES

The body, time, the holy instant, and *miracles* are all learning devices. Ultimately, the body, time, holy instances, and miracles are not necessary. None of these experiences exist in Eternity. Once the Truth is known, what need is there of a learning device? Miracles are reparative (shifts from unreality to Truth) and, therefore, exist only in time. There are no miracles in Heaven. Likewise, there is no forgiveness in Heaven. Forgiveness is a tool for perception corrections. In Heaven, perception need not be corrected. Once we have perfection, that's it! In perfection there is no vacillation, no indecision, no hesitancy—only the movement forward in truth. In the world, we can always make things better. In Eternity, it is already done. Eternity is joy. Nothing needs to be fixed or improved in Heaven. Thus:

When the Will of the Sonship and the Father are One,
their perfect accord is Heaven.

T-3.II.4:6

The body no more dies than it can feel.
It does nothing.
Of itself it is neither corruptible nor incorruptible.
It "is" nothing.
It is the result of a tiny, mad idea of corruption
that can be corrected.

T-19.IV.C.5:2–7

You recognize, however dimly, that God is an idea. . . .
What you find difficult to accept is the fact that,
like your Father, "you" are an idea.

T-15.VI.4:4–5

GOD IS AN IDEA AND YOU ARE AN IDEA

Jesus asks that we join him in "the idea of peace," for "in ideas, minds can communicate." (T-15.VI.7:2). As we realign our minds with the Mind, we move from *mindlessness* to *mindfulness*. We keep ourselves mindless with habituated unconscious activities, with projective thoughts, television, sleep, alcohol, food, and drugs—the list goes on. We have to have food, but we easily overdo eating and thereby get pulled ever more into bodily identification. The most special of all the special relationships we have is the one we have with our bodies. According to the *Journal of the American Medical Association*, 35 percent of Americans are overweight and 34 percent are obese. That adds up to 69 percent of the population. Eating is a decision, and thoughtless (unconscious) eating literally weighs us down, and we feel guilty. Guilt is unbecoming of a Child of God. God is the only Cause.

> Prepare yourself in advance for all the decisions
> you will make today by remembering they are
> all really very simple.
> Each one will lead to happiness or unhappiness.
> Can such a simple decision really be difficult to make?
>
> W-64.5:3–5

> Appetites are "getting" mechanisms,
> representing the ego's need to confirm itself.
> This is as true of body appetites
> as it is of the so-called "higher ego needs."
> **Body appetites are not physical in origin.**
> The ego regards the body as its home,
> and tries to satisfy itself through the body.
> But the idea that this is possible is a decision of the mind,
> which has become completely confused
> about what is really possible.
>
> T-4.II.7:5–9

If we were perfectly awake and we had no guilt buried within, we would not allow ourselves to be caught in any addiction, compulsion (like overeating), or obsession.

> The ego has no power to distract you
> unless you give it the power to do so.
>
> T-8.I.2:1

The ego says *you are a body*, a thing, a person; you have a name, a personality, a history, a résumé, and an identity; and if you let it go and yield to the Will of God, you will disappear. This is nonsense. What do we lose when we lose an illusion? What is to be gained by dreaming?

Why are you unhappy?
Because 99.9 percent of everything you think,
and of everything you do, is for yourself—and there isn't one.
WEI WU WEI (1895–1986), TAOIST PHILOSOPHER

The ego disappears because it was never real to start with. Who are we when the masks are removed? We walk around with a mistaken identity regarding our true selves. Once the main masks (our bodies and our individuality) are no longer there—who are we then?

The purpose of the Atonement
is to restore everything to you;
or rather, to restore it to your awareness.
T-1.IV.3:6

The ego is a broken splinter, a tiny segment of the mind. The Atonement restores awareness of Eternity. The existence of the body *seems to say* that the separation from Heaven has indeed occurred. The experience of the body *seems* to prove the reality of our separation. The ego actually made the body so we would forget that we have a Mind, a Mind that we could use to get us back Home.

The ego made the body with eyes
so it could seek out the semblance of sin.
DR. KENNETH WAPNICK

We might then say that the ego made the body with a tongue so we could complain. We are learning how to use the body as a means for healing, rather than attack. In order to do this, we must reverse thinking. We may think when we overeat that we are giving pleasure to the body; overeating is, however, an attack on the body, and everybody knows it. This produces guilt and depression, as we blame ourselves for our lack of willpower and for overindulging. The answer to what we're looking for (the Peace of God) is not found in this world, and knowing that can lead to despair, unless we are willing to dive deeper past the surface—past the mask—and uncover Life's more profound meaning. We are here to remember God. The goal is to awaken from the dream.

> *Mind creates all things that are,*
> *and cannot give them attributes it lacks,*
> *nor change its own eternal, mindful state.*
> *It cannot make the physical.*
> **What seems to die is but the sign of mind asleep.**
>
> W-167.6:5–6

This is really good news. Nothing dies except something that was never real to start with. Even that cannot die, because it never lived. *It is because we are an idea* (and not a body) *that we can be in full communication* with all that is. The ego would tell us that the body has won, that we are at the mercy of our appetites, hungers, cravings, and desires. It is not true. Which mind are we listening to? The ego says, "You are a body;" that is your home. Spirit says you are the Self that God created and forever His child.

Relinquishing our dedication to death does not mean that we can do away with the body. It certainly does not mean that we can ignore the body or use it foolishly. The body is a learning device, a tool, a vehicle, and a communication device. The best thing we can do is to keep this tool working efficiently until we have learned as much from it as we can and, when the time comes, gently lay it down.

A WORD ABOUT SUICIDE

We can all have great sympathy for those who commit suicide. Suicides are often very sensitive people who have a great deal of trouble living in this world. This *is* an insane world, and adjusting to its many pains and problems can be very difficult. It could be said that from the standpoint of the Course, every death is a suicide, since:

> *No one dies without his own consent.*
> *Nothing occurs but represent your wish,*
> *and nothing is omitted that you choose.*

W-PI.152.1:4–5

Why do some people commit suicide? Is it because they are fed up with the world? Do they do it out of anger or as an attack on others, as if to say, "Look what a bad parent you were. You raised a child who committed suicide." Do they do it because they are suffering from an incurable painful illness—in which case we can certainly have a great deal of sympathy?

The Course is trying to help us get our values straight. There is "nothing outside of you" that has any value. There is nothing of this world, no amount of fame, money, or pleasure, that will ever be truly satisfying. The only true satisfaction comes in doing the Will of God.

Death does not mean that we are going to be instantaneously enlightened or delivered from the ego's thought system. Everything depends on where the mind is. That is why this is a Course in "mind training." Death, presents us with a profound learning opportunity, as death makes it clear that we are not bodies. Thank God for the wonderful hospice centers which now make it possible to "learn how to die."

If you are not a body or a "personality" in the sense of individuality, eccentricities, and so forth, then who are you? Here, indeed, is an opportunity for movement into greater awareness and an awakening to an awareness of our true Self—or not. Everything is always a matter of choice.

There is a risk in thinking death is peace.

T-27.VII.10:3

Peace comes not in leaving this world. Rather, it comes through the practice of forgiveness. Forgiveness undoes our guilt, which is the real cause of all of our anguish and pain, and that is something that can be done right now—here, today. Wanting to leave the world reinforces the seeming reality of the world. We are here to remember—to awaken to the reality of who we really are. In this sense, committing suicide means unlearned lessons may yet remain to be learned. Going back a grade is not a sin. Who know what lesson any individual soul needs to learn? This world is a classroom and the best thing we can do is to learn how to live a happy dream in which we bring our blessing instead of our condemnation on the world. Once we see a forgiven world, we can graduate out of this insanity while living within the world. If we fail to apply ourselves and learn what we are here to learn, suicide can, in this sense, be seen as dropping out of school.

The answer to what we're looking for is not found in the world, and that can bring us a good deal of despair—if we let it. The good news is, as Lesson 138 says, "Heaven is a decision I must make." So we might as well get on with making the decision for Heaven now.

NINE

Beyond the Body

///|\\\

Can you who see yourself within a body
know yourself as an idea?
Everything you recognize you identify
with externals, something outside itself.
You cannot even think of God without a body,
or in some form you think you recognize.

T-18.VIII.1:5-7

In Valladolid, Spain, where Christopher Columbus died in 1506, stands a monument commemorating the great discoverer. The most interesting feature of the memorial is a statue of a lion destroying one of the Latin words that had been part of Spain's motto for centuries. Before Columbus made his voyages, the Spaniards thought they had reached the outer limits of the earth. Thus, their motto was *"Non Plus Ultra,"* which means "No More Beyond." The word being torn away by the lion is "Non" or "no," making it read "Plus Ultra." Columbus had proven that there was indeed "more beyond." And, thus, it is that there is so much beyond what we see and think we know.

God did not make the body, because it is destructible,
and therefore not of the Kingdom.

The body is the symbol of what you think you are.
It is clearly a separation device, and therefore does not exist.

T-6.V.A.2:1–2

Did you ever look at your face in the mirror and wonder how you got into this body, this figure, this form, this frame, this thing that *seems* to define us? Do you ever feel as though you would like to move beyond this body, this skin, and this limitation in form?

You are not limited by the body,
and thought cannot be made flesh.

T-8.VII.14:1

Am I this fleshy thing that stares back from the mirror, a picture, or a video? We think that what is real is on the outside appearing in form. All the while the outside is impermanent, changing, dying, drifting away. Reality remains forever constant. Mind/Spirit/Love cannot be limited to form. Spirit cannot be destroyed, and it can never die.

One summer, Dolores and I were vacationing in upstate New York. Driving around on some backcountry roads, we came upon a Revolutionary War cemetery with an ancient rock wall collapsing all around. No one else was there. We stopped, got out of the car, and began wandering about, reading the tombstones, mostly from the second half of the eighteenth century. Several Revolutionary War soldiers' tombstones had the same inscription on them:

Remember friend, as you pass by,
as you are now, so once was I.
As I am now, so you must be.
Prepare yourself to follow me.

THE EGO BODY

My friend Joe Wolfe, A *Course in Miracles* teacher, tells the story of a mystical event that occurred when he was only three years old, the experience of realizing he was condemned to spend a lifetime trapped in a body.

It was on a farm in Indiana where my first mystical experience occurred. Dad was on the porch of an old farmhouse negotiating the details of the care of my brother, talking with the wife and husband, owners of the farm and parents of the small tribe of kids who happily played amidst the dirt and dust of the front yard.

My brother kept inviting me to join them in play, but I was too busy crying. In fact I was screaming at the top of my little lungs. Something was happening that I couldn't quite comprehend. Looking back at the event, I realize that this brief moment of tears had been the first realization that I was in this body. A flood of comprehension flowed through that three-year-old mind. Not in words or thoughts, which had yet to be developed, but in a knowingness that cannot be described in worldly terms.

The body felt alien and constrained, as if confined in an uncommon and uncomfortable concrete suit of heavy armor. It was a feeling of unnatural confinement. Along with that feeling was the distinct awareness that I had just arrived from somewhere very peaceful, somewhere that felt like home. I had left that home to come here for a reason that I did not understand.

I didn't look forward to what was destined to happen next and for the rest of this life, because in a flash of recognition, I was able to see and experience every moment from that point on. I could "see" every moment to come, every encounter, every person I would ever meet and every experience yet to be lived.

I knew with unmistakable conviction that I was in for a long, rough ride. That's why I was crying. Not unlike what is reported by accounts when one's entire life flashes before one's eyes in an instant, usually during near-death experiences, I could see what is described as the future.

Every encounter, every hardship, every person I would ever meet, and every experience of love and loss, of happiness and misery, in that fleeting instant I could see it all. It was terrifying and that is why I was screaming.

Many years later I would come to another realization; it was the profound knowing that I had chosen this path, this duty, if you will, to fulfill a divine request to share the reality of the truth that a wonderful home exists closer than our breath.

Contemporary mystic, A.H. Almaas, speaks of the "ego body," while Eckhart Tolle speaks of the "pain body." Rarely are we indifferent when it comes to the topic of our bodies. We love them or we hate them. We take pride in them or we are embarrassed by them. Deep inside we know that whatever the body is, it is not who we are; yet, we seem to be wrapped up in it. The body grows, and as it grows we become fixated on the body—thinking that it is who we are, and yet, it is merely part of our experience in space-time. It is almost impossible, however, to deny the body's *seeming* existence in the world (T-2.IV.3:9–11). The body is the embodiment of the thought of separation that is perceived as outside—projected by the mind into physical form. It is a symbol of what we think we are.

The ego uses the body for attack, for pleasure and for pride.
The insanity of this perception makes it a fearful one indeed.

T-6.V.A.5:3–4

THE EGO USES THE BODY AS AN APP

A = *Attack*, P = *Pleasure*, and P = *Pride*. An easy way to remember how the ego uses the body is to think of it as an APP. The ego uses the body for *attack*, for *pleasure*, and for *pride*.

Attack Is Obvious

The ego by definition is projective and always ready to attack. It takes only a little provocation, like someone cutting you off on the road, and the ego will grab hold and take your peace of mind away. Notice how the wish to attack comes into the mind and then almost begs the throat and the tongue for permission to be expressed. I like American actress and comedian, Lily Tomlin's line, "Man invented language to satisfy his deep need to complain." Attack is always made upon strangers; that is, we make people strangers by attacking them. We attack them because we misperceive who they are, thinking they are separate from us. Without the idea of separation, there would be no attack.

Illusions carry only guilt and suffering,
sickness and death, to their believers.
No form of misery in reason's eyes can be confused with joy.
Joy is eternal.

T-22.II.3:1, 3–4

Pleasure Is Time Bound; Joy Is Eternal

Pleasures last only for the moment. Eating, drinking, sex, whatever the bodily pleasure may be, lasts as long as the experience lasts. Then it is at best a memory and is no longer a part of our present awareness. The pleasure must then be repeated, which opens up both the possibility for the dulling of the senses through overuse and more insidiously the possibility for addiction. Real pleasure comes only in doing God's Will, which is a deep form of satisfaction leading to "Eternal Joy."

In addition to our belief that the body can give us pleasure, we believe it can give us pain. "Pain," the Course says, "is the only 'sacrifice' the Holy Spirit asks, and this He *would* remove" (T-19.IV.B.3:7). Pain and pleasure are both means for making the body real.

Our Second **P** Is Pride

There is an old proverb that *pride comes before a fall*. Pride asserts that we have come into a world separate from ourselves and impervious to what we think. Another *P* word that goes along with "pride" is "power." The ego also uses the body to obtain power. The only true power, of course, is that of the mind in harmony with the Mind of God. Pride cannot be shared, and nothing real can be increased except by sharing. Like mayflies, who live just one day, every body has its moment and then falls away.

> And this unholy instant seems to be life;
> an instant of despair,
> a tiny island of dry sand, bereft of water
> and set uncertainly upon oblivion.

Here does the Son of God stop briefly by,
to offer his devotion to death's idols and then pass on.
And here he is more dead than living.

T-20.VI.11:3–5

OUT OF BODY OR INNER MIND

A distinction should be made between "out-of-body" and "inner-mind" experiences. To be out of the body implies that there is a body that one is "out of." People who have had near-death experiences sometimes talk about being able to "look back" and see their lifeless bodies. This was true for Anita Moorjani and my friend, Cora Yumul. There is often no looking back, however, because there is nothing to look back *at*, nothing to hunger for or lust after. Most folks, especially the old and sick, are very glad to be set free.

I used to call my 1976 experience an "out-of-body" experience. Later, I realized that it was an "inner-mind" experience. Obviously, the body did not die. I lost bodily awareness very quickly, however, and did not realize that I could return to space and time—physicality and history.

The body is an isolated speck of darkness;
a hidden secret room, a tiny spot of senseless mystery,
a meaningless enclosure carefully protected, yet hiding nothing.

T-20.IV.5:2

The body *is* a baffling, bewildering, and often amazing maze of problematic pains and pleasures. The body *is a thought of separation* projected by the mind into form. As the body is the ego's chosen home, the ego tries to persuade the mind that the body is more real than the mind. Another way to say this is that *the body is in the mind; the mind is not in the body.*

I like to think of those trapped in the horror of the Holocaust ecstatically entering into paradise as they raised their hands into the air and arrived together in Heaven, free of the nightmare world of their tormenters and the hell they created for them. Think what joy to find that nothing had been lost except for hell itself.

> *You are not really "lifted out" of it [the body];*
> *it cannot contain you.*
> *You go where you would be, gaining, not losing, a sense of Self.*
>
> T-18.VI.13:4–5

Even lightweight bodies are heavy, restrictive, and isolating. Losing the body is often spoken of in near-death experiences as being like taking off old, worn-out clothes, only more so. The experience is one of pure freedom.

The body is *a symbol* and a witness to the reality of the "outside"—that which seems to be isolated and separated from the Mind of God. The body is *a belief to be undone* so that what we really are can be revealed to us.

> *The body is a limit imposed on the universal*
> *communication that is an eternal property of mind.*
> *But the communication is internal.*
> *Mind reaches to itself.*
> *It is **not** made up of different parts,*
> *which reach each other. It does not go out.*
> *Within itself it has no limits, and there is nothing outside it.*
> *It encompasses everything. It encompasses you entirely;*
> *you within it and it within you.*
> *There is nothing else, anywhere or ever.*
>
> T-18.VI.8:3–11

*For the body **is** little and limited.*

T-15.IX.5:5

WHEN WE DREAM AT NIGHT, WHERE IS THE DREAMER?

When one sleeps and dreams, one is both the observer and the dreamer of the dream. There is a part of one's self within the dream that is watching the dream about the self. There is objectivity (a perceiving subject and perceived objects), but where does the objectivity come from? Likewise, in near-death experiences, though there is no experiencing body, *something* is seeing; *something* has awareness. What is going on? Our nighttime dreams and daytime dreams have different forms—that is all. Daytime dreams *seem* real because of the seeming reality of the body and the world around us.

The Bible speaks of a new Heaven and a new earth,
yet this cannot be literally true, for the eternal are not re-created.
To perceive anew is merely to perceive again,
implying that before,
or in the interval between, you were not perceiving at all.
What, then, is the world that awaits your perception
when you see it?

T-11.VII.1:4–6

The body is the result of the ego's thought system. Life without beginning or ending is the result of God's thoughts, or the Mind of God. We think we are alive, yet, we dream the world away. In the dream, the world looks very real and Heaven seems like a fantasy. Beyond the dream and the seeming imprisonment of the body—the form, the flesh—we remain very much alive and a part of Heaven even while dreaming we are on a journey Home.

The phrase "I am not a body" appears forty-six times in the Course, since it is repeated as a *Workbook* review. Obviously, this is an important point in the Course. Though bodies seem quite real and though it is almost impossible to deny their *seeming* reality, the fact remains: a body is an image.

> And what are you who live within the world
> except a picture of the Son of God in broken pieces,
> each concealed within a separate and uncertain bit of clay?
>
> T-28.III.7:5

Bodies are often idolized, worshiped, and adored, and the bodies and graves of famous people are revered. In the Catholic tradition, the two most important holidays of the year are the birth of Jesus' body and the death of Jesus' body. Likewise, the bones of a saint are venerated, and yet, a bone is a bone is a bone, and one is of no more value than another. Jesus, speaking in the Course, says:

> I do not want to share my body in
> communion because this is to share nothing.
> Would I try to share an illusion
> with the most holy children of a most holy Father?
> Yet I do want to share my mind with you
> because we are of one Mind, and that Mind is ours.
> **See only this Mind everywhere,**
> because only this is everywhere and in everything.
> It is everything because it encompasses all things within itself.
> Blessed are you who perceive only this,
> because you perceive only what is true.
>
> T-7.V.10:7–12

Like our Father, we are all part of an Eternal Idea, even though the body seems to surrounds us. The skin has its limitations. Minds *can* join; bodies *cannot*. No barriers exist within Mind. Spirit knows no limitations, and we cannot be separated from God except within an illusion. If this corporeal world of form and separation is real, then God is not. If God is real, the dreamworld we *seem to perceive* is not. The outside world, the external manifestation, the very thing that looks so real, *is not*. It is, in fact, going to disappear for each of us. And then we will stand in a Universe so grand there truly are no words for it—only approximations.

> *In most of our human relationships,*
> *we spend much of our time reassuring one another*
> *that our costumes of identity are on straight.*
> RAM DASS, AMERICAN SPIRITUAL TEACHER

Famous people often have very difficult lives, not only because of the perception they have of themselves but also because of the perception the world places on them regarding *who they are supposed to be*. Marilyn Monroe was perceived as a sex goddess by playing into that image; the world played back and reinforced the image, making her seem to be something she neither wanted or could be. As she said it, "You just hate to be a thing."

The Course does not say, "You are more than a body." How could anyone be "more than a body" when no*body* is any*body* to begin with? Jesus is trying to awaken our remembrance of the truth of our existence, not as a body—which will die—but as a Living aspect of the Mind of God—which can never die.

There is no hierarchy of illusions, since all illusions arise equally from the thought of separation. While it is perfectly possible to know the abstract (love and thinking are abstract), the ego body perceives reality as that which is corporeal, physical, and concrete.

To the ego, how the body looks is very important. Just pick up a magazine or turn on the television. The vast majority of ads have something to do with the body—with clothes, cosmetics, jewelry and, more than anything, a host of drugs.

> *A little piece of glass, a speck of dust,*
> *a body or a war are one to you.*
> *For if you value one thing made of nothing,*
> *you have believed that nothing can be precious,*
> *and that you can learn how to make the untrue true.*
>
> T-14.II.1:10–11

A little piece of glass—a diamond, let's say—in which we place great value is just a rock and, thus, as illusionary as are our bodies. The Spanish under the leadership of Francisco Pizarro, in the sixteenth century, destroyed the Incan civilization—for what? For their gold? What is gold but glittering rock on which we place great value? Cosmologists have found a white dwarf star in the constellation Centaurus, which they have nicknamed "Lucy" after the Beatles song "Lucy in the Sky with Diamonds." This white dwarf star is a diamond that weighs 5 million trillion trillion pounds. That is, a diamond that equals 10 billion trillion trillion carats. I don't quite know what a billion trillion trillion is. What value is this diamond? Nothing! In the same way, many of the luxuries and comforts of life are distractions, part of the outside world we make real and worship.

> *Would you, for all these meaningless distractions,*
> *lay Heaven aside?*
> *Your destiny and purpose are far beyond them,*
> *in the clean place where littleness does not exist.*
>
> T-23.IN.4:5–6

There is a story about a man who is very fervent in his prayers, and he keeps imploring God to speak to him. Finally, one night God appears to the man in a dream, and the man tells God that there is something he would like to take with him when he goes to Heaven. God says, "No, you can't bring anything. No one can bring anything to Heaven." Night after night, the man prays and pleads and pleads and begs. Finally, God gives in and says, "Okay you can bring one suitcase, but that is all."

Immediately, the man goes out and sells everything he has. He buys several gold bars and puts them in a suitcase next to his bed. Then comes the day when the man dies, and he shows up at the pearly gates with his suitcase. There he meets Saint Peter, who says, "You can't bring that suitcase in here." The man responds, "But I have permission from God; go ask him." Saint Peter asks God and God answers, "Oh yes, I did make that one exception, but you must look inside the suitcase before he can bring it in." So Saint Peter tells the man, "Okay, you can bring it in, but I have to see what's inside first." The man opens up the suitcase. Saint Peter looks inside and exclaims, "You brought paving stones!"

The belief that you could give and get something else,
something outside yourself,
has cost you the awareness of Heaven and of your Identity.

T-18.VI.2:3

Lesson 130 from the Course says, "It is impossible to see two worlds." The only "thing" that can transition between this world and Heaven must already be a part of Heaven—only the Mind, only Spirit, only Love can transition from the illusory world into Eternity. There is nothing illusory about Heaven. The choice is simple: either we choose illusion or we choose reality.

IT'S NOT ABOUT ANYTHING EXTERNAL

God did not make the body or the material world. Everything material is destructible. The mind that belongs to Spirit, which God created, is Eternal and indestructible. Nothing real rusts or rots, decays or decomposes. Nothing that turns from one form into another is real or Eternal. Plato held that truth is an abstraction (Idea) apart from the material and concrete world of Form. Indeed, the only thing that is real and Eternal is that which is formless: like Ideas, Love, and Spirit.

Form can be diminished; formlessness cannot. God is formless; love is formless; thoughts are formless; ideas are formless; Spirit is formless. Because Spirit is *formless*, we can give and give and give and never lose. Feeding, bathing, and dressing the body, exercising and taking care of its health, takes lots of time. As we grow in awareness, the needs of the body and its many seeming demands become less important, and we see the body and the world as a classroom in which we are seeking to remember Eternity. The only value the body has is revealed through understanding how it is being used—whether for separation or for communication and joining at the level of Mind.

Do you know who your great-great-grandfather was? Maybe there is a name on a family tree with a date of birth and a date of death, but who was that really? A couple of hundred years from now, it is likely that no one will know that we walked around on this planet. Does it make any difference? We are mind first and ultimately (which means now) not a body at all.

The real world is not like this.
It has no buildings and there are no streets
where people walk alone and separate.
There are no stores where people buy
an endless list of things they do not need.

It is not lit with artificial light, and night comes not upon it.
There is no day that brightens and grows dim.
Nothing is there but shines, and shines forever.

T-13.VII.1:1–5

WHERE IS THE MIND?

Universally, folks who have near-death experiences report being able to see at 360 degrees. There is no "back of the head." In my own experience there was no back; there was no head; and yet *something saw* and *knew* and even now *remembers*. What sees when there are no eyes? What hears when there are no ears? What *knows* when there is no ego in possession of the mind? Anita Moorjani in *Dying to Be Me* said that free of the body she was more acutely aware than ever before, and the sharpness of her perception was more intense than it would have been had she been able to use her poor body.

Mind cannot be made physical, but it can be made manifest
"through" the physical
if it uses the body to go beyond itself.
By reaching out, the mind extends itself.
It does not stop at the body,
for if it does it is blocked in its purpose.

T-8.VII.10:4–6

We are trying to get our values straight. We are trying to get Home to God by letting go of our attraction to the physical, the mundane, and the valueless. If you want to get Home, if you want to return to a place you never left, bet on Mind; bet on Spirit. Bodies always die. In this world and the next, Spirit always prevails. The body is nothing without the Spirit that gives it Life. It can only do what the Mind directs.

Beyond the body, beyond the sun and stars,
past everything you see and yet somehow familiar,
is an arc of golden light that stretches as you look
into a great and shining circle.
And all the circle fills with light before your eyes.
The edges of the circle disappear,
and what is in it is no longer contained at all.
The light expands and covers everything,
extending to infinity forever shining
and with no break or limit anywhere.
Within it everything is joined in perfect continuity.
Nor is it possible to imagine that anything could be outside,
for there is nowhere that this light is not.

T-21.I.8:1–6

TEN

Why Wait for Heaven?
Awakening from the Dream of Death

Why wait for Heaven? It is here today.
Time is the great illusion it is past or in the future.
Yet this cannot be, if it is where God wills His Son to be.
How could the Will of God be in the past, or yet to happen?
What He wills is now, without a past and wholly futureless.
It is as far removed from time as is a tiny candle from a distant
star, or what you chose from what you really want.

W-131.6:1–7

The dictionary definition of eternity is "a state or place of timelessness." Time, like the body, is a great illusion, and *eternity*, according to the quotation that begins this chapter, is "as far removed from time as a tiny candle from a distant star." Time cannot be a part of eternity any more than a body can occupy space in Heaven.

The changelessness of Heaven is in you,
so deep within that nothing in this world but passes by,
unnoticed and unseen.
The still infinity of endless peace surrounds you

gently in its soft embrace,
so strong and quiet, tranquil in the might of its Creator,
nothing can intrude upon the sacred Son of God within.

T-29.V.2:3–4

Sometimes I'll ask at a workshop, "How many of you would like to go to Heaven right now?" Very few raise their hands. And yet deep inside we know that right now is all there is. No one wants to go to Heaven *right now* because we are so attached to our ego/body identity. Becoming aware of the Kingdom of Heaven does not mean we must drop our body. That will happen in its own good time. Indeed, according to the Course, the time for that event has been decided already. Being in Heaven means knowing that Heaven is here, now. There is no other time.

I do dimly perceive that whilst everything
around me is ever changing,
ever dying, there is underlying all that change
a Living Power that is changeless, that holds all together,
that creates, dissolves, and recreates.
That informing Power or Spirit is God.
And since nothing else I see, merely through the senses,
can or will persist, He alone is.

MOHANDAS GANDHI (1869–1948)

Time, like the body, passes away. Spirit is timeless; Mind is timeless. Love is timeless: The center of a cyclone is a point of absolute stillness. Around the outside of the cyclone there is an immense amount of chaos, but in the center, everything stops. Think what it would be like to step away from chaos and come into the quiet center, a now place of Eternity where time has stopped. My 2007 experience with encephalitis was very quiet and very peaceful. It was actually several days after I came out of the coma before I had the thought that brought me back to this world—that thought was, *You have bills to pay!*

Time is a trick, a sleight of hand,
a vast illusion in which figures come and go as if by magic.
Yet there is a plan behind appearances that does not change.
The script is written.
When experience will come to end your doubting has been set.
For we but see the journey from the point at which it ended,
looking back on it, imagining we make it once again;
reviewing mentally what has gone by.

W-158.4:1–5

From the central vantage point, we may see chaos whirling around us, and yet, we are not part of it. To step out of the center and back into the world is to step back into activity, movement, time, and chaos. The Course uses a similar analogy of our being above a battleground.

Be lifted up, and from a higher place look down upon it.
From there will your perspective be quite different.
Here in the midst of it, it does seem real.
Here you have chosen to be part of it.
Here murder is your choice.
Yet from above, the choice is miracles instead of murder.
And the perspective coming from this choice
shows you the battle is not real, and easily escaped.

T-23.IV.5:1–7

From within the center of the cyclone, imagine you can step up or down and, thus, into time at any point, in any society, or into any body. If you step back into the world as Hindu, you will see the world through Hindu eyes. If you step back as a woman, you will have a different perspective than that of a man. If you step back into the twenty-first century, you will see things differently than you would in the nineteenth century.

> *God and the soul are not in space-time*
> *But belong to the realms that are intrinsically or*
> *essentially real. Time ends where there is no before or after.*
> *We perceive only a shadow of the real living in a world*
> *created and sustained by our own cognition.*
>
> **MEISTER ECKHART (1260–1327), CHRISTIAN MYSTIC**

> *In the ultimate sense, reincarnation is impossible.*
> *There is no past or future, and the idea of birth into a body*
> *has no meaning either once or many times.*
> *Reincarnation cannot, then, be true in any real sense.*
> *Our only question should be, "Is the concept helpful?"*
> *And that depends, of course, on what it is used for.*
> *If it is used to strengthen the recognition of the*
> *eternal nature of life, it is helpful indeed.*
>
> M-24.1:1–6

TIME, ETERNITY, AND REINCARNATION

I wrote my master's thesis in theology on the work of French pale-ontologist and Jesuit priest, Father Pierre Teilhard de Chardin, and his theory of conscious evolution. I loved Teilhard so much that when I began to understand the Course, I thought at first that I had encountered a roadblock because the Course was not talking about evolution. Fortunately, I had Ken to help me see my way through what at first appeared to be an impasse. We are now moving beyond time. Eternity is a state of perfection and timelessness. Evolution is a time-bound concept, as is reincarnation.

The purpose of time
is to enable you to learn how to use time constructively.
It is thus a teaching device and a means to an end.
Time will cease when it is no longer useful in facilitating learning.

T-1.I.15:2–4

We are already Eternal. Learning takes time. Outside of time there is no learning. Instead of our evolving spiritually over time, we could realize the truth "now" and go Home "now." The *ultimate* goal is the complete restoration of Heaven, and we need do nothing except recognize what is already true. Going Home is, thus, a vertical rather than a linear process. God realization is possible for anyone at any moment. This is why mystics are able to "see all" in an instant. It is simply a matter of re-cognizing what is already there. There is nothing we can do to "earn" our way into Heaven. Once we know we're already there—that's it!

The word "ultimate" appears twenty-one times in the Course and the word "ultimately" appears thirty-six times. Whatever phrase appears after the word "ultimate" or "ultimately," you can be sure it is absolutely true, as in the quotation that ended the previous section: "In the ultimate sense reincarnation cannot be true." Alternatively, we could say that reincarnation is true in time, but seeing how there is no time, it is not true. Let's take this concept a little deeper.

THE OCEANIC QUALITY AND THE WORDLESS WORLD

We noted earlier that one of the primary characteristics of a mystical experience is the oceanic quality, that is, a sense of vastness in which one feels as though there is a merging with one's environment inside and out. As we move deeper into God, we increasingly see that *all experience is open to us.* The concept of reincarnation is then helpful, *if it helps us understand that life is eternal.*

> *I died as a mineral and became a plant.*
> *I died as a plant and rose to animal.*
> *I died as animal and I was Man.*
> *Why should I fear? When was I less by dying?*
> *Yet once more I shall die as Man, to soar*
> *With angels bless'd; but even from angelhood*
> *I must pass on: all except God doth perish*
> *When I have sacrificed my angel-soul*
> *I shall become what no mind e'er conceived.*
> *Oh, let me not exist! For Non-existence*
> *Proclaims in organ tones*
> *To Him we shall return.*

RUMI (1207–1273), SUFI MYSTIC

In my near-death experience of 1976, I compared our current level of awareness to that of an ant's-eye view. Having survived mass extinction, ants have been around since the time of the dinosaurs. There are approximately 1 million ants for every person on earth. All totaled, they weigh as much as all the humans on the earth. Think about this. There are currently 7.4 billion people on earth. Now multiply 7.4 billion by 1 million and you've got a lot of little points of consciousness.

Eben Alexander said of his near-death experience that in the beginning, there was something very primeval, like primitive bacteria, plant, and animal life. He described what he called the earthworm's-eye view, a place he said that was not foggy or distorted but very limited. It was not like being an animal; rather, it was like being something before and below that. In one of my experiences in working with Salvador, I became, for a time, a pig that was wonderfully wallowing around in muck and mud and a chicken that was cackling on a roof. When I came out of my 2007 experience of encephalitis, I did so very slowly, going through childlike stages of growing awareness. Likewise, Anita Moorjani said she experienced a more primitive "time" when she was her now older brothers and older sister. Yet, this memory she said was happening in a "now" moment place of simultaneity.

> *Like many other beliefs, it*
> *[the belief in reincarnation]*
> *can be bitterly misused.*
> *At least, such misuse offers preoccupation*
> *and perhaps pride in the past.*
> *At worst, it induces inertia in the present.*
> *In between, many kinds of folly are possible.*
>
> M-24.1:1–10

Ken once told me that five different people had told him they were reincarnations of Saint Paul. I've heard a number of reports from others who have said they were a disciple of Jesus or a saint of some sort. The idea of reincarnation can also lead to inertia, insofar as we think all we have to do is to *allow fate* to take its course, not realizing that we have a role to play in the decision-making required to return Home.

> *In this world Heaven is a choice,*
> *because here we believe there are alternatives to choose between.*
>
> W-138.1:1

The key phrase in the earlier section on reincarnation is the first one—"In the ultimate sense, reincarnation is impossible." We noted earlier that the body is always remembered or anticipated, but never experienced just "now" (T-18.VII.3:1). The body is "a figure" in a dream fulfilling a function in relationship to the world. We like to talk about the past and who we were in the past in relationship to the present and what we've gone through. Now that nearly everyone carries around a cell phone with a built-in camera, we can record all the "selfies" we want here.

> *Life is what happens while you're busy making other plans.*
> **JOHN LENNON (1940–1980)**

Notice how much time is spent talking about our past or our hopes and fears for the future. In this sense, *time controls us entirely.* Sin is always seen as something in the past, which now has power in the present. The ego, thus, holds on to and dangles sin out in front of us, reminding us of its presence. Sin is always about something that happened in the past, be it forty years, four years, four hours, or four minutes ago.

> *All your time is spent in dreaming.*
> *Your sleeping and your waking dreams have different forms,*
> *and that is all.*
>
> T-18:II.5:12

Time is "a great illusion." Everything in time is a dream. Our night dreams and daydreams are both dreams. We experience life as a dream precisely because it is impermanent—bodies are impermanent precisely because they are part of time. Spirit is, on the other hand, forever real.

> *Spirit is in a state of grace forever.*
> *Your reality is only spirit.*

Therefore you are in a state of grace forever.

T-1.III.5:4–6

You look for permanence in the impermanent,
for love where there is none, for safety in the midst of danger;
immortality within the darkness of the dream of death.

W-131.1:2

I have sometimes joked that dying might be a bit like waking up in the morning, at which point we can turn to our friends and say, "I just had the strangest life." No one has ordinary dreams; we all have strange dreams. And this life compared to the life we awaken to in spirit makes it all seem like a dream. Past lives are, thus, dreams, and so it is (in time) we go from dream to dream to dream. Would it not be better to "wake up" and be free of dreaming altogether? The ultimate goal is Eternity, and in Eternity, there is no time, no reincarnation, and no dreaming.

Eternity is an idea of God,
so the Holy Spirit understands it perfectly.
Time is a belief of the ego, so the lower mind,
which is the ego's domain, accepts it without question.
The only aspect of time that is eternal is "now."

T-5.III.6:3–5

Ultimately, there is no time—no past and no future—only one beautiful Eternal moment. Why go from one life to another life, to another life? If you have experienced several lives, then which one of them is true—your present life or maybe the life where you were a slave, a soldier, or perhaps a saint? If the latter was so, would that one then be more important than the one you are living now, perhaps as an alcoholic? If you were a saint hundreds of years ago, could you not by this time have evolved to a point where you were able to overcome bodily temptation? Why go from dream to dream to dream? Would it not be better to wake up? Once Spirit is free, then we can sing; then we can laugh; then we can be truly joyful; then we can dance!

> *Death is the central dream from which all illusions stem.*
> *Is it not madness to think of life as being born,*
> *aging, losing vitality, and dying in the end?*
>
> M-27:1–2

> *Why do you think of other births?*
> *The fact is, there is neither birth nor death.*
>
> **RAMANA MAHARSHI (1879–1950), INDIAN SAGE**

INFINITE AND UNCONDITIONAL LOVE

Anita Moorjani described being encompassed by unconditional love, and yet even the word "love" did not do justice to what she felt. The Course never uses the word "unconditional." It does, however, speak of Infinite Love, which it equates with Infinite Patience. There was, Anita said, nothing she needed to do to receive the Divine Love that came her way.

> *Infinite patience calls upon infinite love,*
> *and by producing results "now"*
> *it renders time unnecessary.*
>
> T-5.VI.12:3

Dr. Eben Alexander and Anita Moorjani both spoke of a Love that transcends condition. *Total open-mindedness*, the Course says, is perhaps "the last attribute" a teacher of God develops. The Love

Anita felt was *totally undiscriminating.* One need do nothing to earn it. It is simply a matter of acceptance of what is. The ego wants to pick a fight with God. Life is nice when we quit fighting and let God win.

Who among us would want to keep coming back to the confines of a body? No one enjoys trying to live in a body that does not work well or one that is in constant pain. For many folks, this life is a prison and a limitation in form. Who wants to keep the dream, the drama, the soap opera, going? Would it not be better to step out of time and into Eternity?

French philosopher, mystic, and author, Simone Weil (1909–1943), had a profound mystical experience in 1937 while visiting Assisi in Italy. After that she said, "To always be relevant, you have to talk about things which are Eternal." It does little good to talk about things past, often a place of sin and guilt, or to be anxious about some unavailable future.

The Will of God is entirely apart from time.
So is all reality, being of Him.
The instant the idea of separation entered the mind of God's Son,
in that same instant was God's Answer given.
In time this happened very long ago.
In reality it never happened at all.

M-2.2:1–8

Time is linear; it flows from the past into the future. Physicality provides us with an identity in space-time. It is for this reason that this life is a dream and any idea of any prior life a dream as well.

Heaven is here. There is nowhere else.
Heaven is now. There is no other time.

M-24.6:4–6

SECTION IV

Heaven and A Course in Miracles

ELEVEN

The Kingdom of Heaven Is Like. . . Heaven in the Parables of Jesus

There is nothing outside you.
That is what you must ultimately learn,
for it is the realization that
the Kingdom of Heaven is restored to you.
For God created only this, and He did not
depart from it nor leave it separate from Himself.
The Kingdom of Heaven is the dwelling place of the Son of God,
who left not his Father and dwells not apart from Him.

T-18.VI.1:1–4

I used to visit Ken for what I called my "Annual Spiritual Checkup." He was an excellent therapist. I was very lucky, as was anyone who came under his tutelage. One spring day in 1993, Ken and I sat down in the dining room of the Foundation for A Course in Miracles, overlooking the Tennanah Lake in Roscoe, New York. Ken's opening line was, "How is your Kingdom?" Four years earlier, Reverend Diane Berke and I had founded Interfaith Fellowship, and we had recently moved our church into Cami Hall, a piano recital hall directly across from Carnegie Hall in New York City. We were doing quite well, so I said, "Fine. How is yours?" He smiled, chuckled, and said, "I don't have a Kingdom." Ken was a very lucky man.

The correct response on my part should have been "What

Kingdom?" Did he mean my own little kingdom? Did he mean Interfaith Fellowship in New York City, or did he mean the Kingdom of God—the Kingdom we all share? His question was a little test that I failed. Driving home that day, I realized what he was trying to teach—there is no Kingdom but God's. No matter how much we may think of ourselves as separate individuals in charge of our own little kingdoms, God's Will has never changed. The only Kingdom there is, is God's Kingdom, and thank God, we are already part of it.

> *Would you remain within your tiny kingdom,*
> *a sorry king, a bitter ruler of all that he surveys,*
> *who looks on nothing yet who would still die to defend it?*
> *This little self is not your kingdom.*

> T-18.VIII.7:5–6

THE ANTITHETICAL EGO

In recognizing what Heaven is not, we can see more clearly what Heaven is. As the Greek philosopher, Plato, says at the end of his dialogue *Theaetetus*, "Having looked deeply into the nature of knowledge, although we do not yet know what knowledge is, we now know something about what knowledge is not." Plato ends the *Theaetetus* by concluding that knowledge has nothing to do with perception or with the accumulation of facts.

Likewise, Heaven is a state of *Being* or *Knowing* that transcends perception. Eternity is not outside us. It is not in space. It is not in the body. It is not in the brain. It is not in the world. Eternity is not in time, and it has nothing to do with individual egos. My Holy Hell experience showed me very clearly that there is no ego in Heaven. The body as a place of our *embodiment* is antithetical to God/Mind/Spirit.

To understand the meaning of a story, a parable or a myth, we engage in demythologizing. To demythologize is to understand the story behind the story, that is, what the story is saying on a deeper level. A story does not have to be "true" in some literal sense in order for the story to have an impact on the human psyche. What earthly story is ever really true? All stories are fictions, including the stories of our lives.

Almost every parable of Jesus in the Gospel of Matthew begins with the phrase, "The Kingdom of Heaven is like . . ." New Testament scholar, Norman Perrin, writes in his book, *The Kingdom of God in the Teaching of Jesus*, "The central teaching of Jesus focuses on the Kingdom of God. Of this there can be no doubt and no scholar does, in fact, doubt it. Jesus appeared as one who proclaimed the Kingdom; all else in his message and ministry serve a function in relation to that proclamation and derives its meaning from it." The word "Kingdom" suggests a place or a region. However, in the Aramaic, which Jesus spoke, the word "Kingdom" means not a place, but *an act of God*. Not knowing Heaven in its fullness, we are yet in the process of awakening. To be fully awake *is to Know* Eternity, which also means being in Heaven.

HEAVEN IS NOT A PLACE

Thinking that Eternity is in the future keeps us in hell. Jesus' two shortest parables appear together in Matthew 13. They are so short that they are sometimes referred to not as parables but as metaphors. As allegory and metaphor are the best way to explain metaphysical principles: when Jesus spoke to fishermen, he told parables about fishing; when he spoke to lawyers, he spoke of the law; and when he spoke to farmers, he spoke about farming.

> *The Kingdom of Heaven is like a grain of mustard seed,*
> *which a man took, and sowed in his field.*
> *Which indeed is the least of all seeds, but when it is grown,*

it is the greatest among herbs, and becomes a tree,
so that the birds of the air come
and lodge in the branches thereof.

MATTHEW 13:31–33

Mustard seeds are tiny black dots about one millimeter in diameter. Few seeds are smaller than mustard seeds. Orchid seeds are so diminutive, they look like dust. In the time of the historic Jesus, however, a mustard seed would have been the smallest seed that a farmer might have sown. Mustard seeds do not grow into trees; however, giant redwood trees (the tallest trees in the world) come from cones only an inch long, which contain tiny kernels about the size of a tomato seed.

Seeds thousands of years old have been found preserved in clay pots in ancient Egyptian tombs. When watered, planted in fertile soil, and exposed to sunlight, these primordial, dormant seeds came back to life. Life was never really lost to them; it was only dormant, only sleeping. As we have seen, according to the Course, we, too, are sleeping. According to a report by *National Geographic*, a group of Russian scientists uncovered a seed cache of *Silene stenophylla* (a flowering plant native to Siberia) 128 feet below the permafrost. Buried by an Ice Age squirrel thirty-two thousand years ago, the seeds, when planted, came back to life. These seeds were some thirty thousand years older than the seeds found in the Egyptian tombs!

God waits with infinite patience, knowing that we are headed Home. Like the seeds hidden thousands of years ago, we are Eternally retaining the memory of God. Even in the mind of the most hardened criminal, God cannot be shut out. Under the ego's dark foundation lies the memory of God (T-13.III.2:1). While we "dream the world away," the memory of God lies latent like a tiny seed, a little spark, which can, when nourished and given light, come back to Life.

*For the memory of God can dawn only in a mind
that chooses to remember,
and that has relinquished the insane desire to control reality.
You who cannot even control yourself
should hardly aspire to control the universe.*

T-12.VIII.5:3–4

*The miracle but calls your ancient Name, which you
will recognize because the truth is in your memory.*

T-26.VII.16:1

In every soul there remains an ancient memory. We cannot lose our soul, but we can *temporarily* lose awareness of it. Thus, the memory of God lies innately and invisibly growing inside every soul, ever moving toward rebirth. In every soul there remains a hint of something very familiar, a melody, an ageless tune, and the joyful reminiscence of Eternity. No one lives without this memory, and awakening to reality means leaving illusion.

*In many only the spark remains,
for the Great Rays are obscured.
Yet God has kept the spark alive so that
the Rays can never be completely forgotten.
If you but see the little spark you will learn of the greater light,
for the Rays are there unseen.*

*Perceiving the spark will heal, but knowing the light will create.
Yet in the returning the little light must be acknowledged first,
for the separation was a descent from magnitude to littleness.*

T-10.IV.8:1–5

Think of the little spark as your soul and the Great Ray as God. We are a part of God as much as a ray of light is a *brilliant* extension of the sun. I love it when a favorite mystic from long ago uses a phrase we find in the Course. Seven hundred years ago German mystic, Meister Eckhart, regularly used the phrase, "the little spark." Once planted in the mind like a kernel, a seed, or an embryo, it begins to grow, and a little spark begins to shine. The flower possesses its beauty, even though it is still in the seed. The seed must die so the flower can show off its beauty and produce new seeds. Its beauty just has to be drawn out, and light is the key ingredient. Add light and nourishment, and voilà! Another flower.

The word "person" comes from the Etruscan *per*, meaning "through," and *sonar*, meaning "sound." A baby's first cry is a "statement," an announcement of its presence in the world. It comes with the first inhalation and then the cry—the first exhalation. Thus, it is that when someone dies, we say they have *expired*—the breath, the voice, the *expression* has left the body. Laws of creation are reflected in the growth of a seed into a plant, an embryo into a body, or as Teilhard and the Course are teaching us, a thought can lead us to a transformed mind. This mind might not only awaken; it might grow and become a mighty and beautiful flower. You are that flower. Together we form a bouquet.

And be not conformed to this world:
but be ye transformed by the renewing of your mind,
that ye may prove what is that good,
and acceptable, and perfect will of God.

ROMANS 12:2

The spark is still as pure as the Great Light,
because it is the remaining call of creation.
Put all your faith in it, and God Himself will answer you.

T-10.IV.8:6–7

When we descend into the world of form, *we seem to* separate from Eternity by becoming occupants of bodies within this world. We then misperceive the body as "us." This is not a sin and God is not mad at us for running away from Home. God knows the world we now seem caught in is a dream from which we will awaken. It need not be fought against—only seen for what it is.

If the world were perfect, it wouldn't be.

YOGI BERRA (1925–2015), NEW YORK YANKEES CATCHER

There was often starlight truth in Yogi Berra's malapropisms. If the world were perfect, that would be Heaven. As we move in awareness to the acceptance of the reality of the Eternal, so then indeed is earth turned into Heaven. Heaven is a state of perfection. There is no other time or place. There is no other now. We never left Heaven—that would be impossible.

Truth can never be forgotten by itself,
and you have not forgotten what you are.

W-PII.3.2:1

We cannot forget our Home, any more than a seed can forget its mission. We need only offer *a little willingness* to let what is true be true. We are asked to have the faith of a tiny mustard seed, which knows the right thing to do and when to do it. Each of us will get Home again; we will remember Eternity. That is our destiny. The only question is, when? Heaven is a decision we must all make, and there is no reason that decision cannot be made today. Accepting the Truth as true (accepting the Atonement) is the right thing, the real thing, the only thing that matters. It is the only "thing" that will awaken and bring us back to Life.

> *If ye have faith as a grain of mustard seed,*
> *ye shall say unto this mountain,*
> *Remove hence to yonder place; and it shall remove;*
> *and nothing shall be impossible unto you.*
>
> MATTHEW 17:20

Given the right conditions, a mustard seed is "destined" to become a plant; an acorn, a mighty oak; or a small seed from a little redwood cone, an enormous redwood tree. Every soul is destined for Eternity—not as a separated, individualized human being or as a separate body. We are destined for greatness as we come to remember the truth of our reality as Spirit—in this Eternal now.

> *On your little faith, joined with His understanding,*
> *He will build your part in the Atonement*
> *and make sure that you fulfill it easily.*
>
> T-18.V.2:6

Moving mountains is a metaphor for doing something great. In accepting the Atonement, we are not doing something monumental. We are leaving the trivial behind and turning toward Eternal truth. We are moving from fear to Love, from body to Spirit—from earth to Heaven.

When you made visible what is not true
what "is" true became invisible to you.

T-12.VIII.3:1

We made fear visible and Heaven invisible. As we begin to *see* the little spark of Spirit, we learn of the great Light. However, the Great Rays are hidden when the mind is focused on worldly problems. Sparks of Love are ignited from within us, but we are afraid to look directly at the sun (Son), fearful that if we did, we would be blinded. In truth, we would be enlightened. The sun seems so bright, and yet, only by acknowledging the Self can the Truth be known. There were those who said that when they looked into Ken's eyes they saw Jesus. To see the Christ is to see perfect Oneness and to know no other.

Those who see themselves as whole make no demands.

W-37:2:7

In perfect Oneness we see the Self. Seeing the spark within, the mind begins to heal. We then have "in-sights," holy instances, moments outside of time. These insights are *seeds*, which, given a little loving care, can grow into a memory of the Eternal Life.

The Kingdom of Heaven is like unto leaven,
which a woman took and hid in three measures of meal
till the whole was leavened.

MATTHEW 13:33

Yeast is even smaller than a seed, nothing more than a single-celled fungus, which can transform something solid and heavy into something airy and light. This process looks like a miracle. Three measures of meal would have made a lot of bread, but only a *pinch* of leaven is needed to transform a pile of dough into a loaf of bread. In the same way, only *a little willingness* is needed to overlook what is not there.

> *The wind of God's grace always blows upon us.*
> *But, we must raise the sail.*
> **SWAMI VIVEKANANDA (1863–1902)**

The answer to the problems of this world is *always* one of accepting responsibility and living fully in the moment. The "Responsibility for Sight" section from the Course (Chapter 21, Section II) asks us to look at our problems straight on, be honest, and stay awake. Move away from the defense system of denial (sleep) into a more awakened state. Which thoughts will we nourish, and which thoughts will we let go? *Guilt* can drive us into hell, just as the acceptance of God's Will and forgiveness (letting go of the past) brings us Home.

> *The belief in hell is inescapable*
> *to those who identify with the ego.*
> T-15.I.4:1

When a thought is planted in the mind, be it in the *wrong-minded* or the *right-minded*, it begins to grow, and it can become a seemingly mighty thing. A little fear, a little paranoia, or a little grievance is allowed into the mind; or, perhaps, some form of righteous indignation comes galloping along looking for attention, and then there is war. A thought of peace comes by on the wings of a dove and peace can return to earth.

IF YOU'RE GOING TOO FAST, FALL DOWN

My friend and Course teacher, Lorri Coburn, uses the illustration of a sled going down a hill. If you can catch it when it's just pushed off (before it gets momentum), you can stop it, and the tipover won't hurt. If the sled gets going (if it gets momentum), it's nearly impossible to stop without crashing. Or, as Gary Lahti, a member of a local Miracles class, who used to teach skiing, told his students, "If you are going too fast, fall down." Once the decision for war is made, pampered, nurtured, cultivated, and even cherished in the mind, war becomes progressively inevitable. In the same way, the decision for peace can much more economically be nourished, cultivated, and allowed to grow.

Once the seed is planted in the ground, the leaven is placed in the bread; once the little spark or the little light is seen in the mind, a quantitative shift occurs. All that is required is that we be willing to make the choice and follow the Voice for God—then let the seed grow, the leaven rise, the Kingdom of Heaven come into view.

AWAKENING IN HEAVEN

Folks sometimes wonder why the Course does not erase the illusions of the ego thought system more quickly. God cannot control the speed with which we choose to learn. In the opening of the Course, it says that the time we take to learn the Course is voluntary. The curriculum, however, is, as we have seen, *a given*, a gift from God; and it is specific to our individual path of salvation. God created the whole process so long ago that it stands outside of time, thus, making it Eternal. The first step in learning the Course is trusting that the path is true. The first of the ten characteristics of a Teacher of God is trust. This is the first characteristic because all of the other characteristics of a teacher of God rest on trust. We each decide upon the speed with which we will learn and on how willing we will be to follow this perfect plan of salvation. Even plans that are not perfect work, for all failure leads us eventually to success.

Though we are not in charge of the program, there are two

major learning devices we are in charge of—time and the body. Ultimately, they are both illusions. The Holy Spirit knows, however, how to use illusion to awaken us to reality. We are each in charge of the speed of our journey Home, so watch out for the speed bumps and other drivers who honk their horns and flash their lights. Keep growing slowly. No matter how young or how old, we are always headed Home.

TWELVE

Running Away From Home

God is at home, it's we who have gone for a walk.

MEISTER ECKHART

O ne of the best ways to understand the basic message of the
Course and the nature of Eternity is found in Jesus' parable
of the prodigal son. Ken said it might be better to call this parable the Story of the Father's Love. It appears only in the Gospel
of Luke, following the stories of the lost sheep and the lost coin,
and is, thus, the third in a series of parables about redemption and
salvation. It is mentioned twice in the Course. The parable begins:

A man had two sons.
And the younger of them said to his father,
"Father, give me the inheritance that falls to me."
And he divided up his property and gave it to him.
And not many days after the younger son gathered all
together and took his journey into a far country
and there wasted his substance in riotous living.
And when he had spent all,
there arose a mighty famine in that land
and he began to be in want.

LUKE 10:11–14

The father, in the story, is very clearly God. Everyone is the Son of God—or use the word "daughter" if you prefer; it does not make any difference. Spirit has no gender, parts, or gradations, and Life cannot be confined to a body.

L(EARNING) OUR WAY BACK HOME

What is interesting in the story is not so much what the father says as *what he does not say.* There are two important things he does not say. First, the father does not deny his son's request. The third sentence in the prodigal son story is, "And he divided up his property and gave it to him." The father does not say, "Look, maybe we should talk this over. Is this really a good idea, you going off by yourself like this?"

FREE WILL MUST LEAD TO FREEDOM

We cannot be forced to follow God's Will. Freedom from fear cannot be thrust upon us. We must then "l(earn)" our way Home. This is a *course* in miracles. It is specifically designed to help us remember God.

Free will does not mean that you can establish the curriculum.
It means only that you can elect what you want to take
at a given time.

T-IN.1:4–5

God has endowed us with free will because "all loving creation is freely given" (T-2.I.2:8), and it is a joyful experience to be free, just as it is depressing to be confined. Free will has been given to us for our joy. Because we have free will *ultimately,* we will each be led to the realization that there is nothing we want to do more than our Father's Will. In this is our greatest freedom.

> *Truth is God's Will.*
> *Share His Will and you share what He knows.*
> *Deny His Will as yours,*
> *and you are denying His Kingdom "and" yours.*

T-7.X.2:5–7

While adopting the ego may look like free will ("I'll do it my way!"), following the ego is, in fact, a denial of free will, as our will is then subject to the ego's many demands, wants, needs, addictions, obsessions, and compulsions, which are forms of confinement rather than freedom. The difficulty is in thinking we are an ego rather than seeing that the ego is something we made up. What makes the Course unique among spiritualities is that it tells us why we made up the ego-body and the world. We are all prodigal sons and daughters. We have all run away from Home. We are all hiding out in a world of our own making, trying to do things on our own without the benefit of Divine guidance.

THE MESSAGE OF THE ATONEMENT

One of the questions that comes up at almost every presentation on the Course is "How did this whole ego thing get started in the first place?" Very simply put, the message of the Atonement is—it never happened. We never left Home. We are simply dreaming that we did. That dream is the dream of every prodigal son and daughter. In our collective dream, we left Home and we have gone into a far-off country. The realization that we are dreaming enables our finding freedom from the tyranny of the ego.

The Kingdom is perfectly united and perfectly protected,
and the ego will not prevail against it.

T-4.III.1:12

There is nothing sinful in leaving Home. It is a choice we make, not realizing that the "university of hard knocks"—the painful education one gets trying to do things on one's own—will fail, a turnaround will occur, and we will eventually turn toward Home. The "university of hard knocks" would be a better teacher if the tuition (the cost of listening to the ego's voice for separation) were not so high. Life would be easy if we simply followed the Will of God.

Is there anything God cannot do? Yes, God cannot not be God. God cannot be mistaken. God cannot be out of accord with himself. God cannot destroy himself. God cannot die. God cannot be bound by time. God cannot come into a body. God cannot be remembered alone. God cannot inflict His Will upon us. We must *want to* do God's Will, and the only way *to want to do it* is to recognize that it is our own will.

This thing called free will *seems* both a curse and a blessing. When young, we dream of the day we will be able to strike off on our own, getting a driver's license and a car; going on a first date; moving away from home; moving in with a friend; getting a job; taking up a career; and establishing our own home. We each bring with us certain talents. Properly developed, these talents can lead us Homeward. This is the message of another of Jesus' parables concerning the Kingdom of Heaven—the story of the talents, an exhortation to Jesus' disciples to use their God-given talents in the service of God.

- We are happy insofar as we do God's Will, which is our own will.

- We are happy insofar as we invest wisely, thus, bringing joy to the whole Kingdom.
- We are miserable to the degree to which we selfishly misuse what has been entrusted to us.

We take what we have and we venture into a foreign land, there to find our fortune, perhaps to build a little kingdom for ourselves, outside of Heaven. Yet, *inside* everyone knows—*this is not it!* This is not Eternity. This is not a place of peace. This is not a place of safety. This is not a place of perfect Love. *This is not Home!*

The prodigal son wastes his money on *wanton* living. "Wanton" means extravagant, willful, or riotous. In John Bunyan's 1678 classic, *Pilgrim's Progress*, a temptress named Wanton tries to distract our hero, Pilgrim, and take him off his course to his intended destination, the "Celestial City" (Heaven). The ego says, "Come follow me—power, pleasure, and pride all lie this way." Little do we know how lonely power, pleasure, and pride can be. The last words of Nathan Rothschild (1777–1836), perhaps the richest man in the world at the time, owner of a worldwide banking dynasty, were, "Poor unhappy me! A victim to nervousness and fancied errors!—all because of money."*

Having left Home (trying to do things our own way), we are no longer clear about our Father's Will. In many mythological traditions, the hero falls into a deep sleep and this sleep leads to disturbing dreams. We are very good at fantasy, make-believe, and fairytales.

> Children "do" confuse fantasy and reality,
> and they are frightened because
> they do not recognize the difference.

The Last Words of Notable People, by William B. Brahms

The Holy Spirit makes no distinction among dreams.
He merely shines them away.
His light is always the Call to awaken,
whatever you have been dreaming.

T-6.V.4:3–6

Imagine a parent standing over the bed of a child. The child is twitching and turning and it is clear that the child is dreaming. In a similar way God awaits our awakening and return Home. Love, the Course says, waits on welcome, not on time, and our will has power over all fantasies and dreams.

The good news is, we cannot really forget our Father, and we're not really lost, because God has not forgotten us. The world seems so big and filled with many distractions. Fortunately, God has also set up a plan (a GPS system) by which we can awaken and return Home when we grow tired of dreams and the chrysalis of our consciousness begins to stir, and the wish for awakening comes into the mind. We each return Home by our own often circuitous and sometimes convoluted route. Life, however, need not be convoluted. It can, in fact, become increasingly joyous as our will and God's become evermore One.

And when he had spent all,
there arose a mighty famine in that land,
and he began to be in want.
And he went and joined himself to a citizen of that country;
and he sent him into his fields to feed swine.
And he would fain have filled his belly with the husks
that the swine did eat; and no man gave unto him.

LUKE 15:14–16

THE BOTTOM OF THE PIT

The prodigal son would willingly eat what the pigs had to eat. As a youngster on the farm in Missouri, it was my job to slop the pigs, and I assure you, pigs will eagerly devour *anything* edible. We have all ventured into a strange land and wasted our resources, and we found nothing of lasting value—save for Love—the only thing that lasts when all else has disappeared.

> *Tolerance for pain may be high, but it is not without limit.*
> *Eventually everyone begins to recognize, however dimly,*
> *that there "must" be a better way.*
> *As this recognition becomes more firmly established,*
> *it becomes a turning point.*
> *This ultimately reawakens spiritual vision,*
> *simultaneously weakening the investment in physical sight.*
>
> T-2.III.3:5–8

Many of our major spiritual leaders began life under staggeringly stressful conditions. Look at the lives of some of those we regard as the most awake citizens of this world and ask yourself, where did the awakening come from? What hardships did the Dalai Lama go though when he was driven out of his native Tibet? Eckhart Tolle was in a deep state of depression prior to his awakening, sitting on a park bench absorbed in what he called "self-talk." If one does not recognize self-talk, one becomes that self-talk and thinks that is who one is. While Eckhart was contemplating suicide, he suddenly became aware that there was a sane voice within him, which the Course calls the right mind, or the Holy Spirit. American speaker and author, Byron Katie, who teaches a method of self-inquiry known as "The Work," was lying on the floor of a woman's shelter in California, watching a cockroach walk across her leg, when she "woke up" and realized that she was responsible for having put herself on that cement floor in that women's shelter watching that cockroach walk across her leg. No one else had put her there.

In the early 1990s, author Neale Donald Walsch's house burned down, his wife left him, and he was in a car accident in which he broke his neck. Alone and unemployed, he was forced to live in a tent, collecting aluminum cans in order to buy food. He began endlessly and fervently writing questions to God on a legal yellow pad, and lo and behold, he began to get answers that transformed his life and the lives of many millions of his readers.

And when he came to himself, he said,
How many hired servants of my father's have bread enough
and to spare, and I perish with hunger!
I will arise and go to my father and will say unto him,
"Father, I have sinned against heaven, and before you.
And am no more worthy to be called your son:
make me as one of your servants.

LUKE 15:17–19

COMING TO OURSELVES—GOING HOME

Eventually, every ego-bound and desultory path fails. At the bottom of the pit of despair, when it looks like there is nothing left to do, the prodigal son has an epiphany—an aha experience—"And when he came to himself." In this case (we can use a capital "S" for Self), he thought, *I can go Home! I can say to my Father, "Father, I have sinned against you and before Heaven. I am no longer worthy to be called your son, make me one of your hired servants."* This is exactly what he does.

And he arose, and came to his father.
But when he was yet a great way off, his father saw him,
and had compassion, and ran,
and fell on his neck and kissed him.
And the son said unto him,
"Father, I have sinned against heaven
and in your sight and am no more worthy to be called your son."
But the father said to his servants, "bring forth the best robe,
and put it on him; and put a ring on his hand,
and shoes on his feet.
And bring hither the fatted calf and kill it and let us eat,
and be merry,
For this my son was dead and he is alive again;
he was lost and he is found."
And they began to make merry.

LUKE 15:20–24

Again, it is interesting what the father *does not say*. The father does not say, "That's right, you've been a very disobedient young man. But I, a good man, will forgive you." The father does not say a word about where his son went or what he did. All he says is, "Put a robe on him; put sandals on his feet; put a ring on his finger." In other words, his status is being completely restored.

Where we go, what we do, the amount of trouble that we get into—none of that matters. Drugs, alcohol, fame, fortune: all good illusions—pick an illusion. It does not matter what the dream is. All that matters is that we awaken from the dream. Dreams are about the past. We *were* sleeping and *now* we are awake. We *were* dead and *now* there is life; we *were* lost and *now* we are found. That is the only thing that matters!

WE MUST AWAKEN

God does not know about the content of our dreams. There is no need to: *an illusion is an illusion is an illusion.* God does know, however, that someday, we too will experience revelation: *we will awaken and all fear will be abolished.* As we awaken, God greets us (figuratively speaking) with open arms. Nothing is said about where we went or what we did. One of the most important teachings of the Course is that we didn't commit any sins or make any mistakes—we just thought we did. The *mistakes* were the tools for learning. The only thing that matters is, "My son was lost and he has been found. He was dead and he's come back to life."

Because of your Father's Love you can never forget Him,
for no one can forget what God Himself placed in his memory.

T-12.VIII.4:1

Now his elder son was in the field;
and as he came and drew nigh to the house,
he heard music and dancing.
And he called one of the servants
and asked what these things meant.
And he said, "Your brother has returned,
and your father has killed the fatted calf,
because he hath received him safe and sound."
And he was angry and would not go in;
therefore came his father out and entreated him.

LUKE 10:25–28

THE PRODIGAL SON'S BROTHER

We are all prodigal sons. We are all also the prodigal son's brother. We are all also the good son, the righteous son, the one who stays home. We do what we are supposed to do. We work hard. We go to church. We raise our families. We pay our bills. We do not squander our resources.

Still, we are projective, jealous, complaining, and withholding of our love. And yet, the father responds to both sons with equal love. We must find the love inside ourselves and forgive our brothers who have wandered away. We must also forgive the good, those of whom we might be jealous. Everyone is literally our brother or sister, and only in the recognition that we have one and the same Father do we become once again whole.

And he answering said to his father,
"Lo, these many years have I served you,
neither transgressed I at any time your commandment;
and yet you never gave me a kid [goat],
that I might make merry with my friends.
But as soon as this your son was come who hath
devoured your living with harlots,
thou hast killed for him the fatted calf."
And he said unto him, "Son, you are always with me,
and all that I have is yours.
It was right that we should make merry and be glad;
for your brother was dead, and is alive again.
He was lost and now is found."

LUKE 15:29–32

THE RIGHTEOUS SON

The prodigal son's brother whines to his father. "Look here, I've been a good son. I have never disobeyed you." Just like the prodigal son, he, too, has a lesson to learn. True happiness comes only in forgiveness and the recognition that we are all one. Our basic problem is "the authority problem." We told God we wanted to be able to live life on our own terms. God—who *is* Love—cannot stop us in this foolishness. The Atonement, which dissolves our foolishness, cannot be misused, only refused. Eventually, like the prodigal sons and daughters we are, we will decide to return Home—the sooner, the happier.

My friend, Alan Dolit, a Course leader from Oceanside, California, tells a story about when he was twelve and living in New York City; he went with his mother to the amusement park in Coney Island and talked his mother into letting him go into the fun house while she waited outside. He was having so much fun that he forgot about his mother. Only when he started feeling hungry did he remember his mother was waiting for him. Alan was afraid that she would be mad because he had been gone so long.

When he came back outside, she was still there patiently waiting for him. He was really glad to see her. This describes the human condition. We have left our Father's Home to go off on our own and play in a fun house called the world. The world is so big and filled with so many toys that we *almost* forget about our Father. Sometimes, it's not until we get into trouble that we go looking for Him once again. God is not upset with our leaving. In infinite patience He very simply awaits our return.

The fear that the Father will be upset with us is a figment of the imagination—of the ego-mind. God has never left us, and we can never leave Him except as a temporal thought. That which is temporal and changeable cannot be real. This world could be compared to a fun house for some, or a house of horrors for others. Like Dorothy in *The Wizard of Oz*, Alice in *Alice in Wonderland*, or the boy in *The Polar Express*, leaving Home can happen only in dreams. While the ego's course is designed to keep us asleep and dreaming, *A Course in Miracles* is a path of awakening to Truth.

Listen to the story of the prodigal son,
and learn what God's treasure is and yours:
This son of a loving father left his home and thought
he had squandered everything for nothing of any value,
although he had not understood its worthlessness at the time.
He was ashamed to return to his father,
because he thought he had hurt him.
Yet when he came home the father welcomed him with joy,
because the son himself "was" his father's treasure.
He wanted nothing else.

T-8.VI.4:1–4

So let us follow One Who knows the way.
We need not tarry, and we cannot stray
except an instant from His loving Hand.
We walk together, for we follow Him.
And it is He Who makes the ending sure,
and guarantees a safe returning home.

W-324.2:1–4

THIRTEEN

Heaven, Hell, and the World

The ego teaches thus:
Death is the end as far as hope of Heaven goes.

T-15.I.4:13

The Holy Spirit teaches thus:
There is no hell. . . .
The Holy Spirit leads as steadily to Heaven
as the ego drives to hell.

T-15.7:1, 4

Mythology in every religious tradition is made up by mortals struggling to understand the Eternal. It's not surprising, therefore, that much of the way Heaven is perceived is in terms of worldly form. I once read an eighteenth century minister's sermon in which he described Heaven as a place where there are very fine horses and carriages. We are now, hopefully, too sophisticated to think of Heaven as a place where there are fancy automobiles.

My 1976 experience was hellish. I had gone to the core of hell not as a body. There was no *body* there. There was, however, a mind and guilt and the thought that everything had gone horribly wrong. P.M.H. Atwater describes an instance when a boy caught in the throes of a near-death experience begged his father for help, and although the father was trying to help him, the boy thought his father was deliberately not helping. This sent him into a state of panic and, therefore, into hell, which was all in his mind.

Like this young boy, I, too, begged for forgiveness, which was not forthcoming—because it was not needed. But I could not help but beg for it. How can you be forgiven for something you did not do? No one could ever be in danger of losing Eternity. Still, I couldn't help begging for forgiveness, as I did not yet understand that what is projected out and seems to be external is not outside at all. It is literally all in the mind. Life is Thought. God is an idea and you are an idea in the Mind of God.

> In this world Heaven is a choice, because here
> we believe there are alternatives to choose between.
> We think that all things have an opposite,
> and what we want we choose.
> If Heaven exists there must be hell as well,
> for contradiction is the way we make what we perceive,
> and what we think is real.
>
> W-138.1:1–3

God does not forgive because God does not condemn. In order to have forgiveness, we must first have condemnation. What I needed was a new way of seeing. In the end we forgive ourselves for our own misperception. According to traditional Christian theology, souls can be forever trapped in hell. Fortunately, this idea does not hold up in the description of near-death experiences. The ego can drive us to hell by making us afraid that guilt from the past will be brought to the present and we will then be punished. None of this is true. God, knowing only Love, never punishes his children, and:

> *the Self that never left its home in God knows no fear,*
> *nor could this Self conceive of loss or suffering or death.*

W-94.3:7–8

Christian mystic, Giordano Bruno, burned at the stake by the Catholic Church in 1600 for *holding opinions contrary to the Catholic faith* (that the sun, not the earth, was the center of our solar system), said to his executioners, "Perhaps you pronounce this sentence with greater fear than I receive it." Bruno knew the world he lived in was insane, and he was ready to leave it.

> *Love is one.*
> *It has no separate parts and no degrees;*
> *no kinds nor levels, no divergencies and no distinctions.*
> *It is like itself, unchanged throughout.*

W-127.1.3

> *The belief in hell is inescapable to those who identify with the ego.*
> *Their nightmares and their fears are all associated with it.*
> *The ego teaches that hell is in the future,*
> *for this is what all its teaching is directed to.*
> *Hell is its goal.*

T-15.I.4:1–4

HELL AND THE EGO

The birth of the ego is the beginning of hell, as hell is the experience of being separated from God's Love. Nothing is more separate from the Will of God than something that does not exist. The good news is—no matter how horrible the idea of hell may be, it is only a belief—a nightmarish dream. Everyone *will* awaken, and the dream of separation *will* be gone forever, simply because it has already happened, not in time but in Eternity. Every mind is a part of The Mind.

> *Earth can reflect Heaven or hell; God or the ego.*
>
> T-14.IX.5:4

> *As long as any mind remains possessed*
> *of evil dreams, the thought of hell is real.*
>
> M-28.6:2

The ego's encounter with death is hell, as it is the end of the ego. Spirit's encounter with death is freedom from limitation. This is a dualistic world where split minds rule—believing in Heaven and hell. There are lots of wonderful things about this world. Topping the list is love itself. As I write these words, it is a beautiful sunny day. The window is open and I can hear the joyful sound of children at play. Right now, right here in this moment, everything is perfect. This moment is every "now" moment. Truth is true all the time—sometimes it's easier to see it.

WHERE DOES THE MIND GO WHEN WE DIE?

As every experience is a learning experience—if we are open to it—then we go where we need to go, Heaven is here and Heaven is now, but the mind must be ready for it. Some folks hang on to the ego with tenacity—I did. Eventually, however, every soul must let go of illusion so God can win.

The period of disorientation, which precedes the actual transformation,
is far shorter than the time it took to fix your
mind so firmly on illusion.

T-16.VI.5:1

We come into this world as babies, and it takes time to slowly adapt. There is a nucleus of an ego in every infant, and yet the ego has not yet completely taken over; innocence is also there. Soon enough, the demands will appear; arrogance will appear. After the innocence of infancy, there comes the terrible twos.

There is a wonderful story about a little four-year-old girl who gets a new baby brother. After they bring the baby home from the hospital, the little girl asks permission to be left alone with the baby. The parents are concerned she may be jealous and may want to hurt the baby. They tell her she can go into the baby's room on her own and they decide to listen in on the room monitor. The little girl goes over to the baby's crib and they hear her say, "Tell me about God, baby—I'm beginning to forget."

Every child is born a mystic.
Then we take him to the school. The school is the serpent.

OSHO (1931–1990), INDIAN MYSTIC

Very young children, while they certainly develop egos, having so recently come from the infinite, are still more open to the mystical than those of us so well-ensconced in the ways of the world. We love our babies as innocence personified.

We are very carefully taught and we adapt to the perspective of reality given to us by the world, our parents, our schools, our religions, society, television, and everything that comes to influence us. This is not done in meanness; rather, it does come out of fear. Our parents learned from their parents, and they, in turn, from their parents. American transcendentalist, Ralph Waldo Emerson, said that spiritually speaking, we are endogenous creatures. We grow from the inside out. So then must the old and rigid ways like an outer shell inevitably give way to a deeper truth.

> *You never change things by fighting existing reality.*
> *To change something, build a new model that makes*
> *the existing thing obsolete.*
>
> BUCKMINSTER FULLER (1895–1983), PRACTICAL MYSTIC

There remains forever inside something that knows, *This isn't it. There has to be something more.* Awakening from the dream of the ego-body takes time. If we are reluctant to let go of the ego and all its many illusions; if we tenaciously hold on to thinking that the ego is who we are, we will suffer, and it may be hellish, but hell is a state of mind and in no way Eternal.

> *You dwell not here, but in eternity.*
> *You travel but in dreams, while safe at home.*
>
> T-13.VII.17:6

As we awaken, the self "we think we are" disappears just like last night's dream and we are reintroduced to the Self we have always been, free of scary dreams. As we cross the bridge, we see that what is real cannot be lost. Life is always present and everything else is literally nonexistent. All that can ever be lost is the ephemeral, the dream, the outside, the shell, the mercurial material world, which does not contain Eternity.

> *Prepare you now for the undoing of what never was.*
>
> T-18.V.1:1

> *What matters at death is where the mind is*
> *in the time before*
> *death comes knocking on the door.*

We release fear through the recognition of the nonreality of the ego—making the return Home joyous. P.M.H. Atwater found that one in seven of the people she interviewed had hellish experiences, but hell, as in the hell I went through, comes only when we are terrified of losing the forms of our identity—the body, our loved ones, our individuality and our personality; our race, religion, status, and position in the community and the world; our work, our degrees, and all the temporal trappings, which only briefly drape the soul.

> *Brother, take not one step in the descent to hell.*
> *For having taken one, you will not recognize the rest*
> *for what they are. And they "will" follow.*
>
> T-23.II.22

STAYING OUT OF HELL

We descend into hell on earth only so long as we judge, project, and condemn. The ego lives in hell by seeking after sin. Sin to the ego is an act that cannot be forgiven. It leads us to the gallows and demands our death. Sin is equal to separation; that is, the affirmation of an identity separates us from our Creator. There is no unforgivable sin. Sin, like all mistakes, can be corrected. All wrongminded thinking can be made right. A miracle is a change of mind that transforms our perception from the ego's world of sin, guilt, and fear to Spirit's peaceful mindedness.

The seven deadly sins, or vices, as classified by the early church, have been used since early Christian times dating back to just after the Council of Nicaea in 325 CE as a means of educating Christians concerning the human propensity to sin. The phrase "deadly sins" is used as though engaging in any of these "sins" would be fatal to the soul. Each so-called sin is really a form of selfishness and *overdoing* the bounds.

The seven "deadly" sins are *pride, wrath, greed, sloth, lust, envy,* and *gluttony.* Each is emblematic of self-worship, where one's own needs are placed above those of the whole. For each of the so-called deadly sins there is an opposite virtue: for pride, *humility;* for wrath, *patience;* for greed, *charity;* for sloth, *diligence;* for lust, *chastity;* for envy, *kindness;* for gluttony, *temperance.*

Pride is considered the original and most serious of the seven deadly sins and the source of the others. It comes out of selfishness, which is the thought of separation. The ego is weak, easily seduced and addicted, and our minds are highly undisciplined. This is a *course* in mind-training. It takes discipline, commitment, and a willingness to move toward truth. Only the arrogance of the ego gets us into trouble; only the desire to build our own kingdom separates us from God. Only pride makes us think we have more worth than another.

Attack in any form has placed your foot
upon the twisted stairway that leads from Heaven.
Yet any instant it is possible to have all this undone.

How can you know whether you chose the stairs
to Heaven or the way to hell?
Quite easily. How do you feel?

Is peace in your awareness?
Are you certain which way you go?
And are you sure the goal of Heaven can be reached?
If not, you walk alone.

Ask, then, your Friend [the Holy Spirit] to join with you,
and give you certainty of where you go.

T-23.II.22:1–13

God did not create an ego. God did not create a hell. What is not of God is not. How simple can it get? Only an ego can experience guilt. Only an ego can be in hell, and only that temporarily. There is no hell because there is no ego. There is no guilt. There is only Eternal Love. Heaven is sharing.

Except you share it, nothing can exist.

T-28.V.1:10

Yet neither oblivion nor hell is as unacceptable to you as Heaven.
Your definition of Heaven "is" hell and oblivion,
and the real Heaven
is the greatest threat you think you could experience.
For hell and oblivion are ideas that you made up,
and you are bent on demonstrating their reality to establish yours.

T-13.IV.1–3

If Heaven is real, the ego is not. If the ego is not, then Heaven is real. Hell and oblivion are fearful ideas, as the ego is already in a state of oblivion, or nothingness. Its existence is a lie, so it never can exist.

No one who follows the ego's teaching
is without the fear of death.
Yet if death were thought of merely
as an end to pain, would it be feared?
We have seen this strange paradox
in the ego's thought system before, but never so clearly as here.

For the ego must seem to keep fear from you to hold your
allegiance. Yet it must engender fear in order to maintain itself.

T-15.I.4:7–11

The special relationship is a strange and unnatural ego device for
joining hell and Heaven, and making them indistinguishable.

T-16.V.6:1

The ego would teach us that it is possible to find Heaven on earth, and yet, truth and illusion cannot be mixed. Either Heaven is true or the world is true—both are not true. We may seek happiness in the world, but we can never find it outside of God.

The real purpose of the special relationship,
in strict accordance with the ego's goals,
is to destroy reality and substitute illusion.
For the ego is itself an illusion,
and only illusions can be the witnesses to its "reality."

T-16.V.9:4–5

The ego is a "diversion" or a "distraction" away from our primary relationship with God. The special relationship is "a substitute illusion," in which we get so caught up that we simply cannot see Eternity. Everything about this world, all of its commercialism, all of its wars, its many religions, its power plays and manipulations, are distractions that keep us from God.

It [the ego] speaks to you of Heaven,
but assures you that Heaven is not for you.
How can the guilty hope for Heaven?

T-15.I.3:6⁻

GUILT IS HELL

The first and second paragraphs from Lesson 39 from the *Workbook* of the Course begin with the sentence, "If guilt is hell what is its opposite?" Freedom from guilt equals salvation, or Heaven. We cannot separate from God. We can only "think that we can." Although the Holy Spirit is reachable at any time, the ego rules in this world. This world is the opposite of Heaven—Heaven being inside and the world being outside.

> *For this world "is" the opposite of Heaven,*
> *being made to be its opposite, and everything here*
> *takes a direction exactly opposite of what is true.*
> *In Heaven, where the meaning of love is known,*
> *love is the same as union.*

T-16.V.3:6–7

As long as the ego exists, the idea of hell exists. Guilt deprives us of the appreciation of Eternity and, thus, keeps us in hell. Simply put, if we had no guilt, we would not suffer. To be free of guilt, we are simply asked to look at our own darkness.

> **Now no one need suffer,**
> *for you have come too far to yield*
> *to the illusion of the beauty and holiness of guilt.*
> *Only the wholly insane could look on death and suffering,*
> *sickness and despair, and see it thus.*
> *What guilt has wrought is ugly, fearful and very dangerous.*
> *See no illusion of truth and beauty there.*
> *And be you thankful that there "is" a place*
> *where truth and beauty wait for you.*

T-16.VI.10:2–6

"In Heaven there is no guilt" (T-5.II.2:1), thus, in Heaven there is no sin; there is no division; there is no anger; there is no attack; there is nothing that pollutes the mind and wreaks havoc. There truth and beauty abide in loveliness forever. There is no fantasy there and there is no thought of hell.

> *There is no loss.*
> *Nothing is there but shines, and shines forever.*
> T-13.I.7:6–7

While the body dies, *you* can never die, because *you* never were a body. The ego is now and always has been nothing more than a dream, so it is a matter of awakening from the dream of death. If the body and the ego do not exist, death takes nothing away from us.

> *Instead of "Seek ye first the Kingdom of Heaven" say,*
> *"Will ye first the Kingdom of Heaven," and you have said,*
> *"I know what I am and I accept my own inheritance."*
> T-3.VI.11:1–8

AFTER BODY OR AFTER LIFE

The world's religions hold to an amazing variety of beliefs regarding what we call the afterlife. A host of different interpretations of Heaven and hell are projected onto the world. A number of the world's different religions describe Heaven as an idealized earth, with flowing fountains, and birds and butterflies fluttering by while sweet music is being played. Some see Heaven as a place where bodies are rewarded with even better bodies, and these bodies are rewarded with the best of "earthly" pleasures, amusements, and delights.

Love is one. It has no separate parts and no degrees;
no kinds nor levels, no divergences and no distinctions.
It is like itself, unchanged throughout.

W-127.1:304

Spirit has no levels,
and all conflict arises from the concept of levels.

T-3.IV.1:6

Each of the world religions has devised complicated and often confusing conceptualizations of Heaven and hell. Mormon theology describes a three-level Heaven, including an upper Celestial Kingdom, which in turn is broken into three different levels. There is a Terrestrial Kingdom reserved for those who believe in the Law of Moses, and a Telestial, or lower level, for those who followed a carnal life on earth; and then hell—a lower level that is a spiritual prison for those who failed to acknowledge Jesus as their savior.

Perception did not exist until the separation introduced degrees,
aspects and intervals. Spirit has no levels,
and all conflict arises from the concept of levels.

T-3.IV.1:5–6

This divided world arose from the idea of separation. There is no hierarchy of illusions. All illusion arises from the thought of separation.

Orders of reality is a perspective without understanding;
a frame of reference for reality to which
it cannot really be compared at all.

T-17.I.4:5

VICARIOUS SALVATION

According to P.M.H. Atwater, the notion that religious tenets determine where we go after death does not match testimonials from the vast majority of near-death accounts. Still, these various doctrines, tenets, dogmas, creeds, superstitions, and beliefs persist, and their influence on humankind is enormous.

> *One illusion cherished and defended against the truth*
> *makes all truth meaningless, and all illusions real.*
> *Such is the power of belief.*
>
> T-22.II.4:4–5

Perhaps the one place where the teaching of the Course and that of traditional Christianity differ most directly is in how the Atonement is understood. In traditional Christianity, the Atonement refers to the pardoning of original sin through the death and resurrection of Jesus. There is a church in a town near where we live that proudly displays a sign that reads, "We preach Christ crucified." According to the Course, the Atonement comes simply in our realization that separation from God never occurred. No one ever sacrificed anything and Jesus went to the cross not to "pay for our sin." Rather, he went to the cross to show us that death is nothing.

> *Eternity is one time, its only dimension being "always."*
>
> T-9.VI.7:1

A teacher was testing the children in her Sunday school class to see if they understood the concept of Heaven. According to the doctrine of her church, one could get into Heaven only if one had accepted Jesus as one's personal savior.

She asked her class, "If I sold my house and my car, had a big garage sale and gave all my money to the church, would that get me into Heaven?"

"No!" the children answered.

"If I cleaned the church every day, mowed the yard, and kept everything neat and tidy, would that get me into Heaven?"

Again, the answer was, "No!"

Now she was smiling. *They're getting it!* she thought. "Well then, if I was kind to animals and gave candy to all the children, and loved my husband, would that get me into Heaven?" she asked.

Again, they all answered, "No!"

She was just bursting with pride for them. "Well," she continued, "then how can I get into Heaven?"

A five-year-old boy shouted out, "You gotta be dead!"

According to Catholic theology, there is a wide variety of states after death, only one of which is Heaven. These include:

1. *Purgatory*—an intermediate state in which one undergoes purification in order to achieve the holiness needed to enter Heaven.

2. *Limbo of the Fathers*—a place for those who lived before Jesus and, thus, could not enter Heaven until Jesus first made it possible for them through his sacrificial blood and his death on the cross.

3. *Limbo of the Infants*—a place for those who died unbaptized and, thus, have not been freed from original sin.

There are then two levels of hell:

4. *The Hell of the Damned*—the place where the wicked are destined to spend eternity.

5. *Hades*—a very deep abyss that is used as a dungeon of physical
   torment and suffering.

Many descriptions of hell see it as a place where *bodies* are constantly being tormented with pain—being burned, frozen, or torn
into pieces. How many times can a body be tortured to death? Many
of the ideas of hell come out of one's culture, even one's geogra-
phy. In Tibetan Buddhism, for example, which developed in the
Himalayan mountains, hell is a dark, frozen plain surrounded by icy
mountains and continual blizzards, where people live naked while
shivering, teeth chattering. All of these various interpretations of
Heaven and hell see pleasure and/or suffering as something related
to what happens to a body. As we have seen, a central teaching of
the Course is that you are Spirit.

Whatever is true is eternal, and cannot change or be changed.
Spirit is therefore unalterable because it is already perfect,
but the mind can elect what it chooses to serve.

T-1.V.5:1–2

The mind belongs to Spirit, which God created and which is,
therefore, Eternal and indestructible. We are mind and, ultimately
(which means now), not a body at all. Heaven is a state of mind and
not a place at all.

In Heaven there is no guilt,
because the Kingdom is attained through the Atonement,
which releases you to create.
The word "create" is appropriate here because,
once what you have made is undone by the Holy Spirit,
the blessed residue is restored and therefore continues in creation.

What is truly blessed is incapable of giving rise to guilt,
and must give rise to joy.

T-5.V.2:1–3

UNIVERSALITY

Heaven is "an awareness of perfect Oneness." In perfect Oneness, judgment is impossible. Universality includes revelation and a deep, collective knowing. Sharing this universality involves nothing but gain. *Ultimately,* only one-mindedness exists. *Ultimately,* only Heaven is real. *Ultimately,* there is nothing outside of Heaven. Only within an illusory dreamworld could we envision a world outside of Heaven.

It is your will to be in Heaven, where you are complete and quiet,
in such sure and loving relationships that any limit is impossible.
Would you not exchange your little relationships for this?
For the body "is" little and limited,
and only those whom you would see without the limits
the ego would impose on them can offer you the gift of freedom.

T-15.IX.5:3–5

FOURTEEN

How to Get Into Heaven

Why wait for Heaven?
Those who seek the light are merely covering their eyes.
The light is in them now.
Enlightenment is but a recognition, not a change at all.
Light is not of the world,
yet you who bear the light in you are alien here as well.
The light came with you from your native home,
and stayed with you because it is your own.
It is the only thing you bring with you from Him
Who is your Source.
It shines in you because it lights your home,
and leads you back to where it came from and you are at home.

W-188.1:1–8

The title to this chapter sounds a little like something you
might find in a popular inspirational magazine, but read on.
This really is about *getting into* Heaven.

Bishop Fulton J. Sheen had a popular television show from 1951
to 1957 called *Life Is Worth Living*. The program was so popular
that he won an Emmy twice for the Most Outstanding Television
Personality. He once told a story about himself. He was to address
a large audience at a major lecture hall in Philadelphia. He left his
hotel room early and decided to walk to the lecture hall. He took a

couple of turns and then realized he was lost. He stopped some boys on the street and asked them if they knew how to get to the lecture hall. They told him. The boys asked him why he was going there and he told them that he was going to tell people how to get into Heaven and he asked the boys if they would like to come along. The older of the boys said no—they thought not. If he couldn't find the lecture hall, he probably did not know how to get to Heaven either.

THE TWILIGHT ZONE

Another favorite television series, *The Twilight Zone*, which ran from 1959 to 1964 and was written and produced by Rod Serling (1924–1975), provided interesting paradoxes and twists and turns in the perception of reality. Often we find that the main character has been dreaming and nothing has happened except within the main character's mind. Rod Serling was known for his deep, gentle voice. You can almost hear him saying something like, "We are going down a road in a place called space-time; we are crossing a bridge from an artificial fantasy world returning to a place we never really left—a place called Eternity."

> *Across the bridge it is so different!*
> *For a time the body is still seen,*
> *but not exclusively, as it is seen here.*
>
> T-16.VI.6:1–2

It is admittedly very difficult for us to talk about life beyond the body simply because we are so tied to the body. The body may be filled with youthful hormones—testosterone and more—or it may be aging rapidly and now filled with aches and pains; either way, it all seems very real, and yet as we have seen, we are not bodies. A story I like to tell at funerals is the story of the dragonfly grub. It goes like this:

THE STORY OF THE DRAGONFLY GRUB

Once, in a small pond, in the muddy water under the lily pads, there lived a little community of dragonfly grubs. They lived a simple and comfortable life in the pond, with few disturbances and interruptions. Once in a while, sadness would come to the community when one of their brothers would climb the stem of a lily pad and would not be seen again. Then, one day, one little dragonfly grub felt an irresistible urge to climb up that stem. However, he was determined that he would not leave forever. He would come back and tell his friends what he had found at the top.

When he reached the top and climbed out of the water onto the surface of the lily pad, he was tired, and the sun felt so warm, that he decided to take a nap. As he slept, his body changed, and when he woke up, he had turned into a beautiful blue-tailed dragonfly with broad wings and a slender body designed for flying. So, fly he did! And as he soared, he saw the beauty of a whole new world far superior to the way of life he had known before. Then he remembered his friends and he wanted to go back to tell them and explain to them that he was now more alive than he had ever been before. His life had been fulfilled, rather than ended.

But now he could not descend below the surface of the water. He could not get back to tell his friends the good news. Then he understood that their time would come, when they, too, would know what he now knew. So he raised his wings and flew off into his joyous new life!

Once you have crossed the bridge,
the value of the body is so diminished in your sight
that you will see no need at all to magnify it.

For you will realize that
the only value the body has is to enable you
to bring your brothers to the bridge with you,
and to be released together there.

T-16.VI.6:4–5

BRIDGE TO THE REAL WORLD

Section VI of Chapter 16, "Bridge to the Real World," from the Course provides one of the best descriptions in the Course of the process of awakening from the dream of death and the rememberance of Heaven. We are on a journey Home, and until we get Home and, therefore, free of the body, the world, and time, we'll go through a variety of steps and stages. Having crossed the bridge into this world, we get absorbed in the world, in time, and in our various stories.

This "is" an insane world, and do not underestimate
the extent of its insanity. There is no area of your perception
that it has not touched, and your dream "is" sacred to you.
That is why God placed the Holy Spirit in you,
where you placed the dream.

T-14.1.2:6–8

This is a world where sin, guilt, and fear seem real, and defenses of all sorts are called for. The thought system of the ego takes us away from Home, away from truth, and deeper into illusion. We might think of this world as a Hollywood version of Heaven. The ego does not want us to know the Truth. If we did, the ego's star would go out. Something is needed to reawaken the mind. Having crossed the bridge into this world, we have fallen into a sleep of forgetfulness, the dreaming of the world, and the unwillingness to remember God's Love.

Sometimes I forget that this is all a dream.

ALICE, IN LEWIS CARROLL'S *ALICE'S ADVENTURES IN WONDERLAND*

The bridge to Heaven does not have a form, though it's difficult for us to think of a bridge and not realize its profound symbolism. Believing we are bodies only means we have fallen into a state of mindlessness. Once we get caught in the body and the world, we lose sight of the bridge, and yet, the bridge enables us to cross "the little gap" that exists between ourselves and God.

Anita Moorjani said she looked back at her body, but that is not true in most cases. In my 1976 and 2007 experiences, I had no awareness of the body until I began to *regain awareness* of the body. Everyone goes through this process as they wake up in the morning, though we don't think about it. Awakening in the morning seems natural, and it is. We may have been off in some strange dream-world, and now we think nothing of the dream. Coming back from a near-death experience is, of course, much more meaningful. After all, your experience is that you *really have been gone.* Often, all you can to do is sit and stare.

THE LITTLE SPARK AND THE GREAT RAY

Think of the little spark as the soul or that part of God in each of us, which cannot be lost. This little spark *is in the mind* and is capable of enlightening the mind—given permission to do so. Think of it like an eternal flame, like a pilot light on a stove, which, given the opportunity, could come fully into flame—*whoosh.* Think ever so slightly like the Holy Spirit thinks and the little spark can become a blazing light that fills the mind.

The little spark is attracted by the Great Ray. Think of God as the Great Ray, which is attracted to the little spark (the soul). Imagine this connection as a great white light, like a filament—a web, a beam of light that reaches down to the soul. As long as the outside dominates the mind, we are temporarily outside of Heaven, and the Great Ray is experienced only as a little spark in the mind. As we move away from the ego, that light grows brighter and brighter.

When it says, "The only value the body has is to enable you to bring your brothers to the bridge with you, and to be released together there," the Course is reinforcing the idea that we are all one and until we see that there is no difference between us, until we love our neighbors *as* ourselves, we cannot be fully aware of the Kingdom.

And with Him,
you will build a ladder planted in the solid rock of faith,
and rising even to Heaven.
Nor will you use it to ascend to Heaven alone.

T-18.V.2:7–8

As Eternity is a state of mind, we can enter Eternity simply by changing our mind and give up on seeing this world as filled with troubles and, thus, hell on earth. Hell is an idea that we made up, and the ego is bent on demonstrating the reality of hell by seeing hell wherever it looks.

My brother is my savior.
Let me not attack the savior You have given me.
But let me honor him who bears Your Name,
and so remember that It is my own.

W-288.1:7–8

MEET YOUR SAVIOR

The way we see our brothers and sisters determines how we cross the bridge and how we can free ourselves of a hell of our own making. We do not—indeed, we cannot—get into Heaven on our own. Metaphorically speaking, in order to get into Heaven, on one side we are holding the hand of someone who is helping or has helped us, and on the other side, we are holding the hand of someone we are helping. I don't know whom you may be helping but I can tell you who is helping you. Take a moment and think of someone you do not like or someone you mistrust. That is your savior!

> *If you perceive truly you are cancelling out misperceptions*
> *in yourself and in others simultaneously.*
>
> T-3.II.6:5

To see Eternity, I must reverse the decision I made to see my brother as sinful and see his innocence instead—thus, it is that I find innocence in myself, and, thus, am I set free. If I truly forgive, I find that I am the one who is forgiven. The ego thought system of sin, separation, and death is a lifeless illusion. Thus, it is our task to awaken from "the dream of death," differences, division, war, and more.

> *Only "your" thoughts have been impossible.*
> *Salvation cannot be.*
> *It "is" impossible to look upon your savior*
> *as your enemy and recognize him.*
>
> T-22.II.11:1–3

If I think anyone is undeserving of God's Love, that *seeing* blocks my own vision. I am not seeing clearly. To see into Eternity, I must have "perfect vision." Perfect vision heals all the mistakes that any mind has ever made. If I exclude anyone from the Kingdom, I exclude myself.

> *Heaven is the home of perfect purity,*
> *and God created it for you.*
> *Look on your holy brother, sinless as yourself,*
> *and let him lead you there.*

> T-22.II.13:6–7

> *Forsake not now your brother.*
> *For you who are the same will not decide alone nor differently.*
> **Either you give each other life or death;**
> *either you are each other's savior or his judge,*
> *offering him sanctuary or condemnation.*
> *This course will be believed entirely or not at all.*

> T-22.II.7:1–4

The Course can, at times, seem a little heavy-handed. It is uncompromising on its insistence that we can't have just a little bit of Heaven. We need to "go all the way." The Course asks us to leave no dark spot hidden in the mind that might hurt us. In other words, in order to *know* Eternity, we have to do a complete cleansing of all hatred, all bitterness, all anger, and resentment.

> *Would you stand outside while all of Heaven waits for you within?*
> *Forgive and be forgiven. As you give you will receive.*
> *There is no plan but this for the salvation of the Son of God.*
> *Let us today rejoice that this is so, for here we have an answer,*
> *clear and plain, beyond deceit in its simplicity.*

> W-126.6:2–5

If you are wholly willing to leave salvation to the plan of God
and unwilling to attempt to grasp for peace yourself,
salvation will be given you.
Yet think not you can substitute your plan for His.

T-15.III.1

This is one of the most important concepts in the Course. The very first words in the Course are "This is a required Course," meaning there is no better plan than God's plan. There cannot be a substitute plan. The ego would have us substitute its plan for God's plan—not realizing that God's plan is our plan and *only* by following God's plan can we be happy.

We can't bring any rubbish into Heaven. Our brothers and sisters are all equal to us. If you can't accept that at this moment, then *simply trust* that this is true, and if you see an attacking thought arise, ask the Holy Spirit to help you be free of that thought—no matter how much you believe it to be true. Only in this way do we know freedom and release from the heavy chains that hold us captive in this sometimes beautiful, very divided world. Heaven is One—there is no division.

Let no dark cloud out of your past obscure him from you,
for truth lies only in the present,
and you will find it if you seek it there.

T-13.VI.5:4

Reason will tell you
that there is no middle ground where you can pause uncertainly,
waiting to choose between the joy of Heaven
and the misery of hell.
Until you choose Heaven, you "are" in hell and misery.

T-22.II.7:7

The phrase "reason will tell you" appears on nine occasions in the Course. Reason is like a muscle. It must be exercised to be strong. Reason is juxtaposed to insanity. No one in his or her right mind would ever leave Heaven. Jesus constantly appeals to our "reasonableness." Reasonableness tells us that all people are equally loved by God. There is no other way we can "see" our way into Heaven.

> *If you attack error in another, you will hurt yourself.*
> *You cannot know your brother when you attack him.*
> **Attack is always made upon a stranger.**
> *You are making him a stranger by misperceiving him,*
> *and so you cannot know him.*
>
> T-3.III.7:1–4

There are no strangers in Heaven. Heaven, by definition, is a state of perfection, and we cannot know our own perfection until we are willing to honor everyone who was created like us. God would not keep us out of Heaven. We keep ourselves out until such a time as we know perfect Oneness. If I have anything against any brother or sister, I cannot yet see Oneness.

> *Sin is a block, set like a heavy gate,*
> *locked and without a key, across the road to peace.*
> *No one who looks on it without the help of reason*
> *would try to pass it.*
> *The body's eyes behold it as solid granite,*
> *so thick it would be madness to attempt to pass it.*
> *Yet reason sees through it easily, because it is an error.*
>
> T-22.III.3:2–5

If I see sin in my brother, I block my own sight of Heaven. There is more innocence and wholeness in our brothers and sisters than we can imagine. The ego is focused not on the light; rather, it looks for even the smallest error, which it affirms as sin.

> *Everyone must be part of your love;*
> *otherwise, no one is part of your love.*
>
> DR. KENNETH WAPNICK

> *Let no dark cloud out of your past obscure him from you,*
> *for truth lies only in the present,*
> *and you will find it if you seek it there.*
>
> T-13.VI.5:1–4

Nancy Sears, a student in our local Miracles class, tells the story of having the oil in her car changed at a filling station some thirty-four years ago. The attendant who serviced the car did not screw the cap back on the oil pan securely. When they got their car back, Nancy and her then young daughter decided to take a ride up into the hills to look at the fall foliage. As she drove up into the Catskill Mountains, the cap on the oil pan jiggled loose, the oil spilled out, the motor froze up, and the car was ruined. When she complained about what had happened to the garage owner, he refused to acknowledge any responsibility for her loss. She was angry and she felt she had good reason to hate this man—he had taken advantage of her. For years thereafter, the man's name and face remained frozen in her mind as objects of hate.

Thirty-four years later, Nancy decided to sign up for a class on defensive driving in order to lower her auto insurance premium. When she got to the class, she recognized the teacher as the man who had refused to accept responsibility for her loss. However, now, for more than thirty years, she had been studying the Course, and as she looked at the man, she saw only his innocence, and any residual hatred she had for him instantly melted away. Nancy forgave the man who caused her to lose her car. She did it automatically and without thinking. Why? The Course had become so much a part of her way of thinking that forgiveness was automatic. She did not have to think about it.

Remember the wonderful story of *Les Misérables?* Bishop Myriel entertains Jean Valjean, an ex-convict, in his home. When he leaves the bishop's home, Jean Valjean steals the bishop's silverware. He is arrested and brought back to Bishop Myriel, who tells the authorities that the silverware was not stolen but was given to Jean Valjean. In fact, the Bishop tells Valjean that he forgot to take the candlesticks as well. Just as God does not see us as guilty sinners, so, too, Bishop Myriel refused to see Jean Valjean as guilty or deserving of punishment. He saw the goodness within, and thus saved Jean Valjean's life. The ego is set to find problems—all the difficulties in the world—and then to project them onto the world, which makes an insane world real in our own eyes.

> *The bridge itself is nothing more than a transition*
> *in the perspective of reality.*
> **On this side, everything you see is grossly distorted**
> **and completely out of perspective.**
> *What is little and insignificant is magnified,*
> *and what is strong and powerful cut down to littleness.*
>
> T-16.VI.7:1–3

This side is the outside, the world of the body and of form. Heaven, being formless, does not have a side. Heaven does not take sides. Because it is Eternal, there is no beginning and no end. "What is little and insignificant is magnified"—that is, the world itself and our position in the world, our status, our pride, and our prominence.

One evening, after a Sunday dinner with Dolores and our adult daughter, Sarah, we sat down to watch television together. There was a show on called *Victoria's Secret Fashion Show*. It was being presented live from Las Vegas. It showed shapely, long-legged, well-tanned models wearing the most exotic, erotic, and expensive underwear in the world, walking up and down a red carpet with angel-type wings strapped to their backs. The models were, thus, referred to as Victoria's Secret Angels. Some of the top bands in the world were playing for the event. See how the outside is magnified, while love, the most powerful force in the universe, is cut down to littleness.

> *They chose their specialness instead of Heaven*
> *and instead of peace,*
> *and wrapped it carefully in sin, to keep it "safe" from truth.*
>
> T-24.II.3:7

THE UNIVERSE OF UNIVERSES

The Course uses the word "universe" in two ways:

1. The Universe of Space and Time

This is the world and the greater physical cosmos or universe of which we are a part.

2. The Universe of Universes and the Universe of the Mind

This Universe does not partake of space-time. Cosmologists tell us that only 5 percent of the physical universe is made up of matter. We might think of that 5 percent as the outside. Things like suns, planets, asteroids, and comets are made of matter. The rest, the other 95 percent, cosmologists speak of as dark matter. Although this dark matter cannot be seen yet, it accounts for 95 percent of the universe.

We know it is there because of its gravitational effect on matter. Maybe cosmologists are mistaken in calling this force "dark matter." Maybe someday they will call it something else. "Matter" implies material substance. Maybe we're not dealing with matter; maybe what's holding the universe together isn't matter at all; maybe the real thing is Mind.

> *Remember always*
> *that you cannot be anywhere except in the Mind of God.*
> *When you forget this, you "will" despair and you "will" attack.*
>
> T-9.VIII.5:3–4

Forgetting that we are in the Mind of God, we find ourselves trapped in bodies, in personalities, in space and time; and yet, what is the most real thing in the universe? Is it not God, Mind, Love, and Spirit, all of which is really what makes for Life?

> *What would you see without the fear of death?*
> *What would you feel and think if death*
> *held no attraction for you?*
> *Very simply, you would remember your Father.*
> *The Creator of life, the Source of everything that lives,*
> **the Father of the universe and of the universe of universes,**
> *and of everything that lies even beyond them would you remember*
> *And as this memory rises in your mind, peace must still surmount a*
> *final obstacle, after which is salvation completed,*
> *and the Son of God entirely restored to sanity.*
> *For here your world "does" end.*
>
> T-19.IV.D.1:1–6

When our universe is in harmony with man, the eternal,
we know it as truth, we feel it as beauty.

RABINDRANATH TAGORE (1861–1941), FIRST NON-EUROPEAN
TO WIN THE NOBEL PRIZE IN LITERATURE

HOST TO GOD OR HOSTAGE TO THE EGO

The fear of God is a major obstacle to peace because it looks like—if God wins, I lose. *Ultimately*, God does win, because *ultimately*, all there is, is God. We can dismiss God and the power of the Mind if we do not see ourselves as Divine.

The ego dissociates itself from the Mind of God. It has to, in order to affirm its own reality. All fear is reducible to the misperception that we have the ability to usurp the power of God. How strange it is that we perceive the most powerful force in the universe as though it was separate from us; yet, that is exactly what the ego is—nothing more than something that believes in impossibilities.

The Holy Instant is an instant in which we choose the Holy Spirit instead of the ego. In the Holy Instant, we allow the Holy Spirit to reign in the mind. Choosing for the right-mind, the wrong-mind is automatically excluded. The Holy Instant, thus, is a moment of complete sanity—a moment in which the mind is host to God rather than hostage to the ego. It is a moment in which we look out on the world free of all judgment. From this perspective, there is no sin, no specialness, no world, no body, and no time. Then it is that we hold an awareness of only Heaven.

In the transition there is a period of confusion,
in which a sense of actual disorientation may occur.
But fear it not, for it means only that you have been willing
to let go your hold on the distorted frame of reference
that seemed to hold your world together.

This frame of reference is built around the special relationship.
Without this illusion there could be no meaning
you would still seek here.

T-16.VI.7:4–6

SPECIAL RELATIONSHIPS

A special relationship is any relationship in which we have some expectation about how someone else is supposed to react or behave in relation to us, and when they don't react that way, we become upset with or annoyed at them. This can be something as simple as not liking someone on television or as complex as feeling profound hatred for someone we think has done us wrong.

Whenever you are with a brother,
you are learning what you are
because you are teaching what you are.

T-8.III.5:8

Never forget your responsibility to him,
because it is your responsibility to yourself.
Give him his place in the Kingdom
and you will have yours.

T-8.III.5:11

Going off and sitting in a cave by oneself until one reaches enlightenment only goes as far as how well we respond to each individual we encounter after coming out of the cave. There is only one of us here and the way we treat our brothers is the way we treat ourselves. For this reason, we must do unto others as we would have them do unto us.

The Kingdom cannot be found alone, and you who
are the Kingdom cannot find yourself alone.

T-8.III.6:1

There is nothing you can hold against reality.
All that must be forgiven are the illusions
you have held against your brothers.
Their reality has no past,
and only illusions can be forgiven.
God holds nothing against anyone,
for He is incapable of illusions of any kind.

T-16.VII.9:1–4

We are learning how to be free of this thing we call an ego. The ego would enchain us by making us a slave to the body. We become enslaved to the body when we *think we must* give in to bodily-based desires, which are not of the body at all but of the ego. Nevertheless, we blame the body. And so it is, we *seem* to become a slave to alcohol or overeating or smoking or whatever *seemingly* bodily-based addiction may come our way.

No one is exempt from the Kingdom unless we think they are, in which case we have temporarily exempted ourselves. God has no favorite children, and forgiveness is the miracle that unlocks the door that grants us entrance. If we really forgive, a miraculous thing happens: we realize that it is we who are forgiven. We are the ones who have been liberated. We are the ones who have found entrance to the Kingdom of Heaven.

FIFTEEN

One-Mindedness

//|\\

The Holy Spirit is the Mind of the Atonement.
He represents a state of mind close enough to
One-mindedness that transfer to it is at last possible.

T-5.I.6:3–4

Seeing with Him will show you that all meaning,
including yours, comes not from double vision,
but from the gentle fusing of everything into "one" meaning,
"one" emotion and "one" purpose.

T-14.VII.7:5

We have seen that we all have split, or divided, minds, referred to in the second passage at the opening of this chapter as "double vision." We seem to have a *wrong-mind*, which we call the ego, that would lead us down a selfish, insane path taking us farther and farther away from our Eternal Home. We all also, thank God, have a *right-mind*, which can follow the guidance of God, which leads us to One-mindedness. We want to be following the right-mind, leading us to the "Mind of the Atonement," which through a purification process eventually leads us Home.

When I was seventeen years old, I found a copy of Canadian psychiatrist, Richard Maurice Bucke's *Cosmic Consciousness* from 1901 in our local library. I became excited as I read his discussion of the lives of various individuals who had, he thought, reached higher levels of awareness than that possessed by the ordinary man, including a level of pure mind-to-mind communication.

Then, in college, I read Ralph Waldo Emerson's essay "The Over-Soul," in which he asserted that ordinary human consciousness is exceedingly limited in comparison to the *Knowledge of the Soul*. Emerson was talking about how *we habitually mistake a false self for our true Self*. "All souls," Emerson said, "are connected at a Spiritual level, and we can experience the Over-Soul if we try."

In seminary, I attended a slide and lecture presentation on the work of French Jesuit priest, Pierre Teilhard de Chardin, whom I mentioned earlier. I taught courses on his theology at the New School University in New York City and for the American Teilhard Association throughout the 1970s.

You are not a human being in search of a spiritual experience.
You are a spiritual being immersed in a human experience.
PIERRE TEILHARD DE CHARDIN

THE NOOSPHERE

Teilhard talked about the evolution of consciousness to a higher sphere, or an Omega Point, which we could equate with enlightenment. He originated the idea of the *noosphere* as "a sphere of thought." The word "noosphere" derived from the Greek *nous*, or "mind," and "sphere," as in "atmo*sphere*" or "bio*sphere*." Teilhard described a "net," or a "web," of consciousness, which he saw connecting all minds on a psychic level. A greater number of people, he said, are becoming aware of this interconnected level of consciousness, in part because there are so many of us packed more tightly together.

> *A holy relationship starts from a different premise.*
> *Each one has looked within and seen no lack.*
> *Accepting his completion, he would extend*
> *it by joining with another, whole as himself.*
> *He sees no difference between these selves,*
> *for differences are only of the body.*
> *Therefore, he looks on nothing he would take.*
> *He denies not his own reality "because" it is the truth.*
> **Just under Heaven does he stand,**
> *but close enough not to return to earth.*
> *For this relationship has Heaven's Holiness.*
> *How far from home can a relationship so like to Heaven be?*
>
> T-22.IN.3.

An unholy relationship is *the conviction that we are forever sep-arate and different from each* other because we believe we are sepa-rate from God. In a special relationship we look within, and there we find sin, lack, scarcity, and more. *Whatever differences there are between us are all on the outside; thus, these differences are all superfi-cial.* Just as the ego sees difference and as it makes difference real, so does the Holy Spirit encourage us to make another choice. Behind all external differences we all share the same content.

The phrase "just under Heaven does he stand" from the pas-sage earlier in this section means that although we are not yet in Heaven, we are far enough along that we realize that this world is a dream. We are not yet Home, but once free of special relationships, we are able to stand outside of the dream of separation. When I see that we are all the same, only then do I see that there is no separa-tion, which also means that there is no sin.

> *Think what a holy relationship can teach!*
> *Here is belief in differences undone.*

Here is the faith in differences shifted to sameness.
And here is sight of differences transformed to vision.
Reason now can lead you and your brother
to the logical conclusion of your union.
It must extend, as you extended when you and he joined.
It must reach out beyond itself, as you reached out beyond the
body, to let you and your brother be joined.
And now the sameness that you saw extends and finally removes
all sense of differences, so that the sameness that lies beneath them
all becomes apparent.
Here is the golden circle where you recognize the Son of God
For what is born into a holy relationship can never end.

T-22.IN.4:1–10

Think of the "golden circle" as a circle of light that surrounds the earth, much like Chardin talked about the noosphere. The holiness that we recognize inside ourselves we must recognize in everyone. Teilhard died in 1955, when the most sophisticated forms of communication were the telegraph, telephone, and television. He could not have known that one day we would have an Internet and a World Wide Web—communication he saw happening purely on the level of mind.

My friend, Alan Dolit, suggests that we think of the Course as a lighthouse. The beacon reveals to the boat captain (the decision-maker) where the rocks are, advises him to stay away from them, and even shows a better way to avoid all rocks. But the beacon doesn't prevent the boat captain from steering into the rocks if he is inclined to do so. And the beacon doesn't physically come to his rescue if the boat crashes. The Course reminds us that the individual is responsible for how he or she steers the boat, because the individual is the captain. However, the Course shows us the fastest, safest, and most joyful route to our destination.

DOUBLE-VISION AND HOMESICKNESS

We all suffer from double-vision. We are capable of seeing through the eyes of Christ, and yet we retain ego glasses, which we wear to hide our eyes from the Son. We block true vision and keep it from our sight by hiding in dark and secret places where we "hope" we cannot be found. This whole world is, thus, a hiding place from God.

What could God give but knowledge of Himself?
What else is there to give?
The belief that you could give and get something else,
something outside yourself,
has cost you the awareness of Heaven and of your Identity.

T-18.VI.2:1–3

Having crossed the bridge into this world, we get absorbed in the world and we suffer from homesickness. Within every soul, there is a melancholy longing for our true Home. This dreamworld of separation is a "twilight zone" where sin, guilt, and fear seem real and defenses of all sorts seem necessary. The thought system of the ego takes us away from Home (Heaven), away from Truth, and into illusion.

Sigmund Freud looked deeply into the psyche of man, and there he found profound *denial* and *repression*, all of which he said made us sick. What Freud did not recognize, however, was that this was a sickness of the soul, and the cure could happen only on a spiritual level.

As you let the Holy Spirit teach you how to
use the body only for purposes of communication,
and renounce its use for separation and attack
which the ego sees in it,
you will learn you have no need of a body at all.

In the holy instant there are no bodies,
and you experience only the attraction of God.

T-15.IX.7:2–3

As long as *we seem* to inhabit a body, the body can serve us as "a framework for developing abilities" (T-7.V.1:1). We must decide how this framework will be used, remembering always that the body's primary function is communication, and what we are to communicate—at all times and in all places—is Love. This we do in great part through the simple process of forgiveness or through simply doing nothing at all—by not projecting—by not creating special relationships that separate us one from another.

Healing is the result of using the body solely for communication.

T-8.VII.10:1

Unnatural thinking is attended with guilt because it is based on the belief in sin, or separation. Communication is "the only *natural* use" for the body. "To learn to communicate correctly" means keeping the ego's manipulative meddling out of the mind, the mouth, the lips, and the tongue.

Ask yourself honestly,
"Would I want to have perfect communication,
and am I wholly willing
to let everything that interferes with it go forever?"

If the answer is no,
then the Holy Spirit's readiness
to give it to you is not enough to make it yours,
for you are not ready to share it with Him.

And it cannot come into a mind that has decided to oppose it.
For the holy instant is given and received with equal willingness,
being the acceptance
of the single Will that governs all thought.

T-3.VI.4:1–5

OMNISCIENCE, OR THE OCEAN OF KNOWING

Our minds are like teaspoons dipping into the vast ocean of the One Mind. We seem to know so little, and yet given the opportunity of opening up to the vastness of the One Mind, we find that we already know all there is to be known. Remember Bonnie McKim's description (in Chapter 2) of her mystical experience sitting on her bunk on a boat on the Mississippi River? She said she had an "Awareness of 'All Knowledge'" and an awareness of the Unity of her Self "with all people, animals and plants . . . even to a blade of grass." Time and time again, various individuals, whom we call mystics, slip into this vast ocean of knowing. Coming to this experience can happen to anyone, anytime, in the journey beyond the ordinary mind.

With Him, you will build a ladder planted in
the solid rock of faith, and rising even to Heaven.
Nor will you use it to ascend to Heaven alone.

T-18.V.2:7–8

WE ARE NOT ALONE

One of the common themes in near-death experiences is that *we are not alone*. As awareness grows, it grows through the process of connecting, joining. No one gets into Heaven alone. As my friend, Course teacher and author, Alan Cohen, said one day in an email, "As I move on in orbits and experience, I value more and more my connections with my friends and peers. Spiritual brotherhood becomes more and more meaningful." This must be true for us all. Who among us does not truly love the connectedness that comes in honest, open sharing? Our greatest joy comes in falling in love because it is an experience of complete sharing and joining with another.

> *The ego would lead us bit by bit*
> *Deeper and deeper into an abyss*
> *Away from Home into loneliness.*

> *Who has need for sin?*
> **Only the lonely and alone,**
> *who see their brothers different from themselves.*
> *It is this difference, seen but not real, that makes*
> *the need for sin, not real but seen, seem justified.*

> T-22.IN.2:1–3

Again, If you're a baby boomer (or even if you're not), you might remember singer/songwriter, Roy Orbison's first great hit, "Only the Lonely," in May of 1960. I had just broken up with my high school sweetheart when that song came out, and I found the song heart-wrenching.

The more we sincerely follow any spiritual path, the more we know we are not alone. We cannot be alone. The Holy Spirit is forever present, ready to guide us Home. The more aware we are of God's presence, the greater our joy and the more we want to do what God is asking of us.

> *God, Who encompasses all being,*
> *created beings who have everything individually,*
> *but who want to share it to increase their joy.*
> *Nothing real can be increased except by sharing.*

That is why God created you.
Divine Abstraction takes joy in sharing.
That is what creation means.

T-4.VII.5:1–4

Anita Moorjani said that it was *not that she "saw"* her father; she talked with him telepathically by being one with him. In my 1976 encounter, I experienced what I referred to as a magnificent merging of multiple minds with those I had always known and now re-membered.

Salvation must reverse the mad belief in separate thoughts
and separate bodies, which lead separate lives
and go their separate ways.

W-100.1:2

The word "image" is always perception-related,
and not a part of knowledge.
Images are symbolic and stand for something else.

T-3.V.4:6–7

Although we are not bodies, it is hard to talk about mind-to-mind communication without some *imagery* of people or intelligent beings. Here are examples of reports from near-death experiences that describe contact with others:

I was surrounded by other beings
who I felt as though I recognized.
These beings were like family, old friends,
who'd been with me for eternity . . .

There was an explosion of love and joy on
seeing each other again.

JEFFREY LONG, MD, *EVIDENCE OF THE AFTERLIFE*, PAGE 11

Their excitement at seeing me, at welcoming me,
was overwhelming.
I felt so loved. I had never felt such a deep sense of belonging.
They radiated profound joy at seeing me.

DALE BLACK, *FLIGHT TO HEAVEN*, PAGE 107

When the Will of the Sonship and the Father are One,
their perfect accord is Heaven.

T-3.II.4:6

BEINGNESS

It is hard to "imagine" life beyond the body, so the mind looks for an image—a statue, maybe, or a painting—something to hang on to. What is described in the connectedness that transcends our earthly selves is not so much a person as *Beingness*, which transcends personhood and individual identity. Beyond the body, there is a Self that we are, a state of Beingness in which the mind is in constant communication with all that is real (T-4.VII.4:3–4). Beingness is like the vast ocean. It is not cut up into little parts. It is simply Oneness.

In the ego's version of Heaven, we get to keep our individuality.

DR. KENNETH WAPNICK

THE MEMORY OF GOD COMES TO A QUIET MIND

This is where the ego gets scared, as there is no individuality in the Godhead. To the ego, the memory of God is terrifying. The memory of God, the Course says, "comes to a quiet mind." Therefore, the ego makes every attempt to see to it that the mind is never quiet—always it will be kept busy worrying. It is only by letting go of the little self that we made up that it is possible to remember the greater Self. We have free will, and we are, each and every moment, exercising that free will. Or you could say that we are *always* at choice. Whose "will" will we observe—the ego's (which we *think* is our own will) or the Voice for God, or the Holy Spirit (which *is* our will)?

I have assured you that the Mind that decided for me is also in you,
and that you can let it change you just as it changed me.
This Mind is unequivocal, because it hears only one Voice
and answers in only one way.

T-5.II.10:1–2

THE THINKING OF THE UNIVERSE

It's interesting to see which lines are repeated over and over again in the Course. It is also interesting to come across a powerful line that appears only once. The last line of Lesson 52 is a review of Lesson 10. The following line, which appears only once in the Course, is something we are to say to ourselves.

Would I not rather join the thinking of the universe
than to obscure all that is really mine
with my pitiful and meaningless "private" thoughts?

W-52.5:7

Think about this. There is a kind of thinking that the Course calls the "Thinking of the Universe" (W-52.V.2:7). We are a part of that "thinking," that "thought." We can't help being part of it. We can, however, get so involved in our "pitiful and meaningless 'private' thoughts" that we have, it seems, no awareness of the great Mind of which we are a part. We could speak of this great Mind as the One Mind, or One-Mindedness, a Whole Mind or a Holy Mind—a state of mind that, though invisible, is completely knowable. Words like "Eternity," "God," "Love," and the "Mind" refer to an invisible reality independent of space and time.

> *The Thoughts of God are far beyond all change,*
> *and shine forever. They await not birth.*
> *They wait for welcome and remembering.*
> *The Thought God holds of you is like a star,*
> *unchangeable in an eternal sky.*
> *So high in Heaven is it set*
> *that those outside of Heaven know not it is there.*
> *Yet still and white and lovely will it shine through all eternity.*
> *There was no time it was not there;*
> *no instant when its light grew dimmer or less perfect ever was.*

T-30.III.8:1–7

> *The universe is awake. It is we who have been sleeping.*
> P.M.H. ATWATER, *DYING TO KNOW YOU*

We go from here into a silence where the language is unspoken and yet understood.

What we have is mind-to-mind communication occurring without words.

Their language has no words,
for what They say cannot be symbolized.
Their knowledge is direct and wholly shared and wholly one.
How far away from this are you who stay bound to this world.
And yet how near are you,
when you exchange it for the world you want.

W-129.4:3–6

THE VOICE FOR EVERYONE

In many near-death experiences, people describe talking telepathically in a universal language. Here is the way my friend, Scott Cleaves, from Tucson, Arizona, describes his experience of *revelation*: "The Voice for Everyone did not speak in a language that I recognized. In fact, I'm not sure it was speaking in a language at all, and yet all the listeners understood it." By listeners, I think Scott meant the One Mind. There is a saying among those who sell lotto tickets: "You have to be in it to win it." In order to be a part of the "Thinking of the Universe," it is necessary to realize that one is already in it. We all know this in simple intuition.

God does not understand words,
for they were made by separated minds
to keep them in the illusion of separation.

M-21.1:7

In my 1976 near-death experience, I encountered a language I described as math-music, with a melodic quality beyond anything imaginable in the best of our symphonies. From the time of the ancient Greeks onward, man has spoken of the Music of the Spheres.

Here is Rod Chelberg, MD's, description of One-Mindedness:

I had another beautiful meditation today that I wanted to share with you. These experiences are so profound! I am finding it easier to cross over into the light within and I can stay there longer. This light is so strong and beautiful. I feel tremendous peace and love. There is no thought of a body anymore only that I know it is there as a vague memory. My mind is so still that there is the absence of any thought at all but there is the experience of being this light. And this light stretches as far as I can see. I am glad that these meditations are getting easier. At my deepest point where there is no thought but love, my heart rate is very slow and I am barely breathing. Oh if I could just leave this world and stay in the light!

I then saw my body for a while and there was a pure white aura that extended about a foot from it. My heart area was red. I saw my body as a channel extending love to all that I saw. I wonder if you felt me touch you? I saw you as white with a center area of red in your heart as well and for a while we were connected in mind. Such a deep feeling of peace and love came over me for you. I let my mind expand and I started to see my other friends like this as well. For a moment, we were all one. There is such tremendous healing in this touch. I let my mind expand again to cover the earth but I could not do it. I felt such resistance but the love pervaded, however it was more grey than white. But, I am okay with that. For a few split seconds, this earth knew peace.

Listen—perhaps you catch a hint of an ancient state
not quite forgotten; dim, perhaps, and yet
not altogether unfamiliar,
like a song whose name is long forgotten, and the circumstances
in which you heard completely unremembered.
Not the whole song has stayed with you,
but just a little wisp of melody, attached not to a person or a place
or anything particular. But you remember, from
just this little part,
how lovely was the song, how wonderful the setting where you
heard it, and how you loved those who were there
and listened with you.

T-21.I.6:1–3

SIXTEEN

Dancing with the Divine

The people said to one another,
Let us make a name for ourselves
and let us make a tower whose top will reach Heaven.
And the Lord said, Behold, the people are one,
and they have all one language;
and this they begin to do.
This is but the start of their undertakings
and nothing will restrain them
from that which they imagined to do.

GENESIS 11:1–3

The story of the Tower of Babel appears early in the Bible in Genesis 11. Like the story of Adam and Eve, it is a legendary tale that further explains the split mind and why we have so many different emotions, mores, cultures, ideologies, languages and different ways of thinking, which divide us.

The ego is looking for an identity independent of God. It would like to *make a name for itself*. The clause in the quotation that opens this chapter, "nothing will restrain them from that which they have imagined to do," describes the development of the ego. Building a tower to Heaven—looking for God Mind/Spirit on the "outside" in the world of physical form—is rooted in the ego's sense of selfishness, which makes the illusion of separation seem all the more real.

Time and again, pride is *the* reason we lose our way, becoming distracted by some "thing" in the illusory world of form. Our split minds are "confounded with many languages" (Genesis 11:7), many different ways of thinking separate us. Some belief systems are so powerful their believers are ready to go to war and attack those who believe differently. Thus, we have insanity, and yet the fact still remains that "there is no one in whom the light has gone out completely."

Having lost One-Mindedness, the split mind vacillates unsteadily between *loveless* and *miraculous* channels of communication—fluctuating between ego-dominance and holy instances where reason prevails and the mind is temporarily realigned with the Whole Mind (One-Mindedness).

ALL WORDS ARE PROJECTIONS

A written or spoken word is *thrown out* into the world. Words, especially words spoken in anger and attack, promote separation. Words can also inspire, extend love, and serve as medicine to weary souls. They can even lead us to the door of "knowledge," at which point we transcend words—knowing only Heaven. Folks often return from near-death experiences completely speechless. It was a very long time after I came out my 1976 experience and the coma in 2007 before I could talk. Words seemed strange, like something forced. About all we can say after such experiences is—"Awe!" It was said that the shepherds on the hillside when they saw the angels at the time of the birth of Jesus were filled with awe. What would you say if you saw an angel?

> *You are a perfect creation, and should experience awe only in the Presence of the Creator of perfection.*

T-1.II.2:3

REVERSING THE THINKING OF THE WORLD

We are looking to remove the blocks to an awareness of Love's presence by "reversing the thinking of the world" (W-11.1). Just as there is a type of thinking that is *the thinking of the universe*, so there is a type of thinking that is *the thinking of the world*. The thinking of the world is broadcast on the news every night. Our task remains: to move from projectivity to receptivity, from anger to serenity, from war to peace, and from separation to unity. The Course is clear, and modern science more and more confirms that *mind* is completely independent of a physical brain.

*The brain does not generate thought
any more than a wire generates electricity.*
PAUL BRUNTON (1898–1981), BRITISH PHILOSOPHER

*You believe the body's brain can think.
If you but understood the nature of thought,
you could but laugh at this insane idea.*
W-92.2:1

Radio and television waves fill the air, but we do not know they are there until we turn on a receiver. In the same way, we are all receivers; the question is, do we have our receivers turned on, and are we listening to WEGO or WGOD? God's voice is always speaking to us, offering us direction if we can only (1) hear it and then (2) follow it. The clearer the hearing (receiving), the easier the following:

Only minds communicate.
*Since the ego cannot obliterate the impulse to communicate
because it is also the impulse to create, it can only teach you that*

the body can both communicate and create,
and therefore does not need the mind.
The ego thus tries to teach you that the body can
act like the mind, and is therefore self-sufficient.

T-7.V.2:1–3

PRIVATE THOUGHTS

Private thoughts are thoughts related to guilt, remorse, self-reproach, and shame. Private thoughts include our secret sins and our hidden hates. They make us feel cut off from the whole and serve as blocks to perfect communication and an awareness of Love's presence. Abandoning private thoughts does not mean that we reveal all of our thoughts to the world—the world is not interested. It does mean that we demonstrate a willingness to look at them ourselves with the aid of the Holy Spirit.

There are things which a man is afraid to tell even to himself,
and every man has a number of such things stored
away in his mind.

FYODOR DOSTOYEVSKY (1821–1881), RUSSIAN NOVELIST

There is a level of Mind accessible and knowable to all, but it cannot be known while we hold onto our desires for specialness and our pitiful meaningless private thoughts. Just as our thoughts of separation call to the separation thoughts of others, so do our real thoughts help us awaken others to thoughts of Truth. It is for this reason that the Course is so appealing, and we know its content to be true.

You believe you can harbor thoughts you would not share,
and that salvation lies in keeping thoughts to yourself alone.

For in private thoughts, known only to yourself,
you think you find a way to keep what you would have alone,
and share what "you" would share.
And then you wonder why it is that you are not
in full communication with those around you,
and with God Who surrounds all of you together.

T-15.IV.7:3–5

MIND AT LARGE

There is a type of connection and transmission of information that transcends the deficient limitations of individual egoistic minds. Aldous Huxley, in his wonderful book, *The Doors of Perception* (1954), said that each one of us is potentially "Mind at Large." However, Mind at Large gets funneled down through the ego's reducing valve of the brain and nervous system.

Dr. Rod Chelberg went one day to visit his patients in a dementia dormitory at a nursing home. Looking around, he could see that his patients' minds were caught in a kind of repetitive loop. The egoistic mind works in a similar way, and we can easily get caught in a repetitive, projective circle—actually a form of insanity in which the same old "song," or "story," is played over and over, thus, reinforcing projection and keeping us deaf and blind.

Would you be hostage to the ego or host to God?
You will accept only whom you invite.
You are free to determine who shall be your guest,
and how long he shall remain with you.

T-11.II.7:1–3

A split mind does not know what it wants and is, thus, out of accord with itself. One-Mindedness (being host only to God) is in accord with itself, at peace, and without confusion. One-Mindedness is the Christ Mind, representing a Will that is One with God's (C-1.6.3).

> *Think of the love of animals for their offspring,*
> *and the need they feel to protect them.*
> *That is because they regard them as part of themselves.*
> *No one dismisses something he considers part of himself.*

> T-4.II.4:1–3

ONE-MINDEDNESS AND STARLING MURMURATION

One of the entertainments we enjoyed on the farm in Missouri was watching glistening, cobalt-blue barn swallows doing their agile evening dance out back of the barn. Barn swallows dart about over barnyards in search of flying insects. They fly with fluid wing-beats in bursts of straight flight, quickly executing tight turns and dives, their long, deeply forked tails streaming out behind. Barn swallows build cup-shaped mud nests almost exclusively on human-made structures—thus, the name *barn* swallows. Dozens of them would be flying about with amazing precision, rapidly diving into the barn from a great height and stopping suddenly on a rafter or a nest. Never did one swallow ever collide with another.

Go to YouTube and type in "starlings murmuration," and you can watch hundreds of thousands of starlings in a *murmuration* (a massive flock of birds in flight), performing each evening a very different, incredibly rapid, and intricate airborne ballet. The word "murmuration" comes from the word "murmur," as in the low, continuous sound of a brook or the wind in the trees and so, too, do these birds also sing to each other.

Starlings fly in flocks of tens of thousands, sometimes as many as one hundred thousand birds at once, and form an immense array of

complicated patterns, looking for a moment like a giant whale float-
ing through the air, then looking like a tornado, now perhaps like a
flying saucer, then maybe like a paisley print, and now looking like
only God knows what. The birds make intricate twists and turns,
all within a tiny fraction of a second, and no two birds ever collide.
Similarly, hundreds of thousands of fish can swim, twist, and turn
inside a school or shoal, all *seemingly* responding to one inner Mind,
as though "someone" is giving directions to go left, go right, go
slowly up, and then come diving down. In fact, no one single bird or
fish is giving directions. They are at that time literally of one Mind.

But minds cannot be separate.

T-21.V.3:8

*No two minds can join in the desire for love
without love's joining them.*

T-18.III.7:6

Minds cannot be separate without God's Will, and God does
not will that our minds be separated. As we have seen, it is the
"thought of separation" that gave rise to this world of duality.
Division can happen only within an illusion, and illusions are never
true. Therefore, in Truth, our Minds are One with His. Jesus knew
this; thus, he could say, "I and the Father are one." In like manner,
we are one Mind with Him. This Truth is not something we merely
believe; it is something we *know*.

DIRECT REVELATION AND
MIND-TO-MIND COMMUNICATION

Anita Moorjani and Eben Alexander both spoke of a "wordless
communication" that occurred during their near-death experiences.

Anita experienced what she called "a complete melding of mutual comprehension." In Heaven, there is no separation, no subject-object, no self and other. This thought is frightening to the ego and liberating to Spirit. There is no greater joy than "Being in Love" with all of Creation.

> We cannot join with God or the Holy Spirit
> because we already are one with Him.
> What is required is just the recognition of what is already true.

DR. KENNETH WAPNICK

Direct communication with God was broken when we made another voice (the ego). We are despairing only because we are more familiar with the voice of the ego than we are with the Voice of God. The ego's constant "chatter" keeps us unaware of the natural innocence and grace that characterize the simplicity and unity of the birds or the fishes.

COMMUNICATION AND UNCONDITIONAL LOVE

The words "community," "communion," and "communication" all come from the Latin *com*, meaning "with" or "together," and *unus*, meaning "oneness," "union," "togetherness," "fellowship," and "sharing." There comes in the Holy Instant "an acceptance of a single Will that governs all thought" (T-15.IV.8:6).

Heaven is the awareness of Oneness—direct, perfect, pure, and without fear. The experience of the single Will, or Holy Instant, that "governs all thought" is a mystical experience. When this experience occurs, we have *clear insights* and we become more aware of *synchronicities*, which are not accidents at all but natural movements within Eternity.

Right now (if you can) open the Course to any page, close your eyes, point to a line, and open your eyes. Does that line speak to you? Synchronicities are all about us if we have ears to hear—on the radio, in a magazine or a book, or in the words your brother or sister would share with you.

The Holy Spirit sees the body only as a means of communication,
and because communicating is sharing it becomes communion.

T-6.V.A.5:5

Finding that Spirit (our inner Teacher), listening to His song, following that voice—is all a marvelous dance. It's like the synchronized starlings, twisting, turning, and twirling together. Living a synchronized life is like dancing with the Divine.

By recognizing spirit,
miracles adjust the levels of perception
and show them in proper alignment.
This places spirit at the center,
where it can communicate directly.

PRINCIPLE 30 FROM *THE 50 MIRACLE PRINCIPLES*

The Holy Spirit's function is entirely communication.
He therefore must remove whatever interferes
with communication in order to restore it.

T-14.IV.8:1

PURIFICATION AND PLACING SPIRIT AT THE CENTER

The key to living the Course is in giving permission to the Holy Spirit to help us purify our thoughts, so that we come to hear only the Voice for God. We need only "a little willingness" to see, hear, and know the truth. If I want to completely remodel a house, I first must remove the old wiring and plumbing and then I must put in new, more effective and up-to-date wires, pipes, cables, and other electronics.

In the same way, miracle-mindedness enables us to remove ineffective, ego-based ways of thinking by placing Spirit, rather than the ego in charge of the mind. Once Spirit is in charge, perfect communication can occur, allowing GPS (God's Plan for Salvation) to work smoothly and effectively getting us where we want to go. Very specifically, this is how the realignmentor correction in perception occurs.

> **When the body ceases to attract you,**
> *and when you place no value on it*
> **as a means of getting anything,**
> *then there will be no interference in communication*
> **and your thoughts will be as free as God's.**
>
> T-15.IX.7:1

How do we get to a place where we can have "no interference in communication?" We get there in two ways: (1) ceasing to be *attracted*—and, therefore, *distracted*—by the body and (2) placing no value on the body as "a means of *getting* anything." It is the role of the Holy Spirit to help us remember Truth, not by giving us any "thing." No "thing" is needed, as we already have all that is real—God, Love, Mind, Spirit.

> *To spirit getting is meaningless and giving is all.*
>
> T-5.I.1:7

"When the body ceases to attract you" is a powerful phrase. Think about it. What would it be like to have no bodily distractions or concerns? We are very identified with the body. We *do* think it is who we are. We think that life without a body would be a tragedy. It is a tragedy to loved ones—that is for sure. To those who have lost loved ones, "Keep going." The only way out is through. Sometimes the doorway to Heaven is through hell.

> *This is our first attempt to introduce structure.*
> *Do not misconstrue it as an effort to exert force or pressure.*
> *You want salvation. You want to be happy. You want peace.*
> *You do not have them now, because your mind is totally*
> *undisciplined, and you cannot distinguish between*
> *joy and sorrow, pleasure and pain, love and fear.*
> *You are now learning how to tell them apart.*
> *And great indeed will be your reward.*

W-20.2:1-7

What is "miraculous" about naturally following GPS is that we get the results we want—which is "miraculously" the same thing God wants for us. What could be better than that? With God, it is always win-win, even when it looks like a loss. Synchronicities often occur during life's most dramatic moments, such as an accident or an illness. Sometimes, at moments like these, when perhaps we've not been paying attention, the message can come through clearly and distinctly.

> *Trials are but lessons that you failed to learn*
> *presented once again,*
> *so where you made a faulty choice before*
> *you now can make a better one, and thus escape all pain*

that what you chose before has brought to you.
In every difficulty, all distress, and each perplexity
Christ calls to you and gently says, "My brother, choose again."

T-31.IX.3:1–2

We look to cross the bridge from an artificial dreamworld to the real world, which is not artificial and not part of a dream. We are moving from sleeping to awakening, from body to Spirit, and from fear to Love. The first step is found in freedom from projections, attack thoughts, hurtful habits, and body-based addictions, compulsions, and obsessions.

PHILHARMONIC

The word "philharmonic" means "the love of music." The Greek *philos* means "loving," while *harmonika* means "tuneful" or "skilled in music." I once gave a lecture on mysticism at a church in Arcadia, California, which is not too far from Hollywood. After my talk, a man came up to me and said that he played in the Hollywood Symphony Orchestra. He told me that sometimes something very wonderful happens when all the musicians in the orchestra are playing in harmony—all of the musicians are on note and in tune. When that happens, he said, everyone *knows* that the moment is absolutely perfect. The conductor knows it is perfect, and the audience knows it is perfect. Then, he said, you sometimes get goose bumps all over your body, and you know without a doubt that in just a few minutes the orchestra will receive a standing ovation. This truly is a mutual experience of the *philharmonica.*

I told this story at another lecture, and a dance troupe leader told me of a similar experience that occurred one evening when she was leading a dance troupe on stage. Again the orchestra was playing perfectly. There was a chorus, and they were all perfectly in concert with one another, and the dancers were all "on point."

They were exactly where they were supposed to be, and the flow was amazingly smooth and synchronistic. When the piece ended, the dancers froze together for a moment, looking away from the audience. The dancers were not wearing microphones, and whispering so that only the other members of the dance troupe could hear her, one of the dancers said, "Did you feel that!?"

SECTION V
Coming Into the Home Stretch

SEVENTEEN

The Classroom Called Cancer

///|\\\

Sometimes the greatest miracles come in the ugliest packages.

After twenty-eight years of working as a Protestant minister, I resigned from the United Methodist Church in June of 1989. For the last sixteen of those twenty-eight years, I tried to bring *A Course in Miracles* into the church. Ken kept telling me that I would not succeed, but I persisted because I felt called to the ministry, and I enjoyed the "pastoral" aspects of ministry. Much of ministry is just being nice to people, and that is fun. I naively thought it would just be a matter of time before the church would begin to come around to the Course—but it was not happening, especially on the hierarchical level.

My bishop and district superintendent both made it clear that they were distrustful of anything that was part of the New Age and, therefore, not to be regarded as serious theology. Three months after I resigned from the United Methodist Church, in September 1989, Reverend Diane Berke and I founded a new church, Interfaith Fellowship, in New York City. In March of 1993, we moved our services from the Little Synagogue to the larger Cami Hall, across from Carnegie Hall. In September 1999, we celebrated our tenth anniversary with a hundred-dollar-per-plate fund-raiser dinner with 120 people. Things were really looking up. We started the church from scratch with very little money and ran the church as an entrepreneurial endeavor with a Board of Trustees, a bookkeeper, a secretary, and several part-time helpers.

In early 2000, a new Board of Trustees was established and it was decided that from then on the church would be run strictly by the Board. No longer was the church to be an entrepreneurial enterprise. Many of the new Board members, themselves interfaith ministers, were looking for an opportunity to speak on Sunday morning. A banker became the new president. Over the course of the next year and-a-half, the entire administrative staff was replaced and my speaking schedule over the course of the next three years (2000–2002) was progressively reduced. In order to pay the bills, I increased my teaching load at Marist College and the State University of New York and I began to look for speaking opportunities as a guest minister at other churches on Sundays.

I went to see Ken at his Center in Roscoe, New York, and told him about the changes that had taken place. He asked me who I was now in relationship to the Fellowship and I said that I was now essentially a part-time employee. When I finished, Ken sat quietly for a moment just looking at me. Then, just as Helen used to do when she wanted to tell me something important, he leaned forward and said he was sorry but he thought I would have to quit the Fellowship. I said, "No, no, it's not that bad." He smiled sympathetically and once again he said he was sorry. Once the founder is out, unless that founder has himself or herself trained a successor—it is probably over.

In April 2001, I had a colonoscopy, and was diagnosed with cancer. On May 7, 2001, a tumor the size of a lemon and eighteen inches of colon were removed, along with five cancerous lymph nodes. The doctors were sure that there was cancer in other lymph nodes, and possibly other organs. I am still convinced that everything is part of a Divine plan, even when it doesn't look that way. I'm not saying that things like war and disease are part of God's plan. I'm sure they are part of the ego's plan, and the ego's plan has a built-in self-destruction mechanism—at some point, it will implode. When it fails, God's plan automatically takes over.

Whenever cancer appears, inevitably we ask, "Why me?" After his experience with cancer, my friend, Rabbi Hirshel Jaffe, wrote a book titled, *Why Me? Why Anyone?* When my friend, Rabbi Gelberman, got the news that I had cancer, he called, and the first thing he said was, "This doesn't sound like you." I had to agree. It didn't *sound* like me. No one wants to hear that they have cancer. I've never been afraid of cancer. I never thought it would happen to me. Daddy was terrified of cancer because he watched both his parents die from it.

As much as I understand the Course, I've never claimed to be enlightened. Until we are enlightened, none of us can be sure of how much *stuff* is buried deep inside, how much is "eating" at us. Even "enlightened" beings die from something: Ramakrishna, Ramana Maharshi, and Ken all died from cancer. My most invaluable guide in life, Dr. Robert Weltman, upon hearing the news, asked, "What's been eating you?" According to Louise Hay, colon cancer comes from difficulties in letting go.

> *What shares a common purpose is the same.*
> *This is the law of purpose,*
> *which unites all those who share in it within itself.*
>
> T-27.VI.1

All of my Sunday morning messages were based on the Course, and now other than my occasional monthly visits, there is little mention of the Course at the Fellowship. The general sense was that the Fellowship had lost its way. A committee of members from the church came and asked me to please break away and start another church. Three times they came and each time I said no. I was enjoying being the guest minister at different churches on Sundays and I liked being free of the politics of administration. I would go to a church somewhere, share a Sunday morning message and an afternoon workshop, and then go home free of whatever politics were going on, on the local level.

AN AWAKENING EXPERIENCE:
THE DAY SEEKING STOPPED

Pictures are more clearly seen in the present rather than remembered in the past. The following account is written in the present tense, as I experienced it in the present tense, and it seems more *immediate* to tell it as it occurred and not as something in the past.

I am awake at four a.m. the morning after the doctor gave me the news that the cancer had spread. The anesthesia has worn off and I am wide-awake! I think they give you the "bad news" when you are still in a stupor so it doesn't hit you quite so hard. They want to do another colonoscopy and start chemotherapy. The only light in the room comes from the hallway. My roommate is fast asleep. The curtains are drawn between us. To my left, the window curtains are open and it is dark out. There is a pine tree next to my window, and out past the pines, I can see the hospital parking lot with its lights ablaze. A light fog hangs in the night sky, making the lights look misty. I lay there in the dark, staring at the night sky, thinking about what the doctors said, and think "You could die. Unlike 1976, this time you could *really* die!" Tears come to my eyes, and I am for a moment overwhelmed.

WHAT DOES DYING MEAN?

Maybe the story is played out? I lay there thinking, Maybe I'm going to leave. If so—so what? I am not afraid of dying—in the sense that dying is the end of things—I know better. I have accumulated in the course of this life far too much evidence to the contrary. I imagine that the loss of the body is going to be an interesting adventure. In some ways I am ready to go. The ringing in my ears will stop. I will be grateful for that! A lot of wonderful things have happened, but life at this point is a struggle. I am broke and sick, and tired. Maybe the story is all played out. Maybe it is time to go Home.

Dying means letting go of everything of this world—all hopes and dreams. I begin to let go of all of what you might call "good" things and "bad" things—maybe even whatever it was I thought I was supposed to do with my life. Maybe, I'd already done it. Maybe it doesn't matter.

I decide to take a good look at death—to give up completely, as there might be no other choice. I decided not to "fight" for my body, as people sometimes do in a panicky way when they hear that they have cancer. I am not going to "beg" God to spare my body. That's not real prayer. That is not saying, "Thy will be done." Prayer is a shift in perception, and a changing of one's mind about a situation, rather than changing the situation. What is needed is a change of mind. Either my body is going to survive this or not. If it is my time to go—I am going. I still think I have unfinished business to fulfill. Maybe I am wrong. God knows best.

INTERFAITH FELLOWSHIP AND *MIRACLES* MAGAZINE

Lying there in the hospital, looking out the window at the lights in the parking lot, I decide it doesn't make any difference what happened with the Fellowship. That story, too, has been played out. I let it all go. I drop all expectations. Nothing has to happen, and that is fine. The difficulties we'd gone through over the course of the past year and-a-half pale and fade away. Interfaith is completely out of my hands now. I open A *Course in Miracles* and read Lesson 189—"I feel the love of God within me now."

Simply do this:
Be still, and lay aside all thoughts of what you are
and what God is; all concepts you have learned about the world;
all images you hold about yourself.
Empty your mind of everything you think is either true or false,
or good or bad, of every thought it judges worthy,
and all the ideas of which it is ashamed. Hold onto nothing.
Do not bring with you one thought the past has taught,
nor one belief you have ever learned before from anything.
Forget this world. Forget this course,
and come with wholly empty hands unto your God.

W-PI.189. 7:1–5

I DON'T GIVE A DAMN

I keep letting go. I let go of entanglements, hang-ups, regrets, and remorse . . . all the nostalgia about what might have been . . . relationships that did not turn out better . . . the Methodist Church . . . the belief that anything "had" to happen . . . even everything I am ashamed of. I go deeper and deeper. I take a good look at my secret sins and hidden hates. And then comes the last thing, the biggest thing of all: I even forgive myself for not having done a better job.

Lying there in the dark, I become *empty* in a way I have never been *empty* before. I don't mean to sound crude, but I take a deep breath, sigh, and say "I don't give a damn!" *Whatever will be will be.* It is clearly out of my hands now. I enter into a place of no will—nothing. I am so *nothing.* I am wondering what was it that thinks, walks, talks. I am empty of desire and anger, and I understand, in a way I had previously only understood intellectually, what Buddha meant when he said that the loss of desire is the key to enlightenment. I achieve by this "letting go" some sort of objectivity.

When a man surrenders all desires that come to the heart,
and by the grace of God finds the joy of God in himself,
then his soul has indeed found peace.

BHAGAVADA GITA 3:30

When there's nothing left to lose, we see who we are behind who *we thought* we were. Peace comes when we give everything away— and say hello to Eternity. The one and only truth of anyone lies in the center of their being. So much is extravagance. I am unusually calm—somehow I'm not quite in the body, although I am aware of the body. I simply lose my attachment to it. This time I am not "hurled" into another dimension. Whatever happens is okay. Dying is perfectly acceptable. I say okay to death. I say, "Okay, come get me," and then an amazing thing happens—you know—*You don't die!* You just keep on going.

I know that I don't exist in an individual way. There is no subject and object. There is just Oneness. The Mind that is thinking everything is One Mind outside of time. Realization requires no effort! Seeking is superfluous! Finding can only happen without interference. There are no fears because all fears are concerned with the world. Dying means letting go of all worldly concerns. When you know you are going to die, why worry? We are born enlightened. To try to achieve something that already is, is absurd.

There is nothing to achieve. There is nowhere to go. There is nothing to be done. We are Divine just the way we are. Problems exist only within a dream of separation. Problems do not *actually* exist. Being Eternal, we are everything and nothing. I am that I am! What is needed is to be deeply involved in Life while remaining unattached to the drama. It is important not to try to fix the world or to be unhappy over some piece of brokenness. I can do my little part by loving it—not condemning it. I am happy with what I have. I love Mother; my darling Dolores; my daughter, Sarah; my sister,

Ann; Shanti and my many friends; and I truly love my work. I am very lucky. I think, *You may be broke, but you have so much.* The acceptance of death brings an incredible awareness.

And then, something I never would have guessed happens: an unexpected experience of compassion. Tears come to my eyes and *Love* in all its glory intoxicates my heart. I think of those who unwittingly dismantled the Fellowship and I feel the greatest love for them and thank them for giving me the opportunity of loving them. Everyone did what they thought they were supposed to do— what they thought was best for the Fellowship. I cannot be mad at anyone. As Martin Luther King Jr. once said, "I cannot at heart be the enemy of any man." I love the Course and believe in the Course. Anger is *never* justified. Then I began to laugh and laugh and laugh, —a really uproarious laugh.

> *To know yourself as the Being underneath the thinker,*
> *the stillness underneath the mental noise,*
> *The love and joy underneath the pain,*
> *is freedom, salvation, and enlightenment.*
>
> **ECKHART TOLLE**

WHAT I LEARNED FROM CANCER

Truth is always simple. We always learn really simple things.

1. *Love is all there is.* It's all that matters. The end result of realization of Truth is Love: compassion, and humility, and the love of everything is the love of Self.
2. *We take so much for granted.* The day I came home from the hospital, just watching our cat, Pockets, walk across the deck, listening to our neighbor mow his lawn, and saying grace together around the dinner table brought tears to my eyes.

Someone sent me the following piece for *Miracles* magazine back in the 1990s. I don't know who Arthur Gordon is. There are lots of Arthur Gordons on the Internet, and none of them seemed to be the one I was looking for. His sentiment expressed in the following quote expresses wonderfully what I was feeling when I came home from the hospital.

Sometimes when you are feeling jaded or blasé,
you can revive your sense of wonder
by merely saying to yourself:
Suppose this were the only time.
Suppose this sunset, this moonrise, this symphony,
this buttered toast, this sleeping child, this flag against the sky.
Suppose you would never experience these things again!
Few things are commonplace in themselves.
It's our reaction to them that grows dull.

ARTHUR GORDON

Happiness is one more walk with Dolores. It's one more driving lesson with Sarah, one more lunch with a friend, or one more chat on the phone with you.

3. *When things don't turn out the way we planned, it's still the right thing.* Another way to say this is *Our Life is none of our business.* Life is God's business. The sooner we turn our lives over, the better.

After I came home from the hospital, I did a two-week vegetable juice cleansing fast and I began a daily diet of detox teas along with a long list of vitamins, minerals, and herbs. I also began a thirty-week session of chemo. I think I got cancer just so I could have that experience in the hospital. With all that was going on with the Fellowship, I needed to engage in a deep, total letting go. I needed to step into complete silence. I needed to stop thinking altogether. The only way to do it was to look at death. Something unneeded died that day, never to be born again. After, I felt clean and free. We never lose an experience of the Eternal. It may fade, but being Eternal, it can never be forgotten.

The sage does not retire from life. He retires from unhappiness.
WILLIAM MARTIN, *THE SAGE'S TAO TE CHING*

There cannot be two captains on one ship. I sent in my letter of resignation. Finally it was over. Immediately, a feeling of release and freedom came over me. Nothing fills the soul like freedom. Thirty emails immediately filled my mailbox, saying, "Hurrah!" and "Good for you!" Contemporary mystic, A.H. Almaas, says that to reach enlightenment we must be free of all "entanglements," "embroilments," and "perplexities"—what the Course calls "special relationships." The Fellowship hired a new minister who looked at the position as a job and not an entrepreneurial endeavor. It would have been impossible to have turned it around.

The Fellowship limped along for a year-and-a-half more before closing. I went to the last service in June of 2003 and did a kind of eulogy. I once did a funeral for a nine-year-old boy. You never know how long some "form" is going to last. The Course tells us repeatedly that it is not the form, the frame, the outside, that matters. What matters is what's on the inside. What matters is content and Eternity is "inside" you. I would never have guessed that Ken would lose his body at the age of seventy-one. According to the Course:

The time is set already.
It appears to be quite arbitrary.
Yet there is no step along the road
that anyone takes but by chance.
It has already been taken by him,
although he has not yet embarked on it.
For time but seems to go in one direction.
We but undertake a journey that is over.
Yet it seems to have a future still unknown to us.

W-158.3:1–6

EIGHTEEN

Home at Last—The Big Let Go

🕸

This is what death should be;
a quiet choice, made joyfully and with a sense of peace,
because the body has been kindly used to help
the Son of God along the way he goes to God.
We thank the body, then, for all the service it has given us.
But we are thankful, too, the need is done to walk the world
of limits, and to reach the Christ in hidden forms
and clearly seen at most in lovely flashes.
Now we can behold Him without blinders,
in the light that we have learned to look upon again.

S-3.II.2:1–4

I've decided to let a couple of my teachers end this book—my good friend, Rod Chelberg, MD, and one of my heroes from the past, British novelist and philosopher, Aldous Huxley.

Here is an email from Rod talking about one of his patients who was dying:

> I met Anna when she was nearing the end of her life. She was 73 and had stage four pancreatic cancer. She failed therapy and was now requesting Hospice service. She also wanted to stay at home and be with her family. Anna was a kind and pleasant woman who led a simple life. She had two questions for me. First she

asked me what it is like to die? Second, she said, "I do not believe in God. What will happen to me?"

I told her about the dying process and about the medications that I used. I told her that she will fall into a very restful sleep and a few days later, her body is going to cease to function. I said, "You will never know it. As you drift off, you will feel an incredible lightness of being. You will float some as you disconnect from your body. You will be very peaceful. I will make sure that you do not suffer any pain or fear."

For her second question, I answered, "As you enter your final days of your life, Christ will be here for you to take you home. In the meantime, you are going to start to remember that you are a thought of love in the mind of God. Love is your true essence. God is not found in churches, but only in your heart where you feel love."

As I explained this to Anna, a variety of white orbs filled the space above her bed. They were thoughts of love. They were angels who came to help her find her way home. Anna looked at me when I was done talking while her daughter softly cried. Then, Anna had a beautiful smile on her face and she said, "You promised me peace and now I have it."

Over the next few weeks, I would visit Anna to see how she was doing. She was always happy and peaceful. She had no fear and no pain. In the last week of her life here, I saw Christ standing on the right side of Anna's bed as a red aura. He radiated love, peace, and contentment. He was patiently waiting for Anna to let go of her body so he could help guide her home. During this time, Anna's daughter placed a vase of variegated red and white tulips on a table next to her bed.

After several weeks, Anna passed away on a sunny Saturday afternoon. She had been unresponsive for several days, but woke up Friday morning and was lucid for two hours. She said goodbye to her family and friends. Then she fell asleep never to wake again. During this time, the tulips by her bed all opened up.

I was at home when Anna's family called me. After I hung up, I raised my arms up and I asked Christ to take Anna home for me. Immediately, I saw Anna's pure white aura enter my dining room on my left. Her face was perfectly clear and peaceful. Christ escorted her by me as she blew me a kiss. She was radiant in light and joy. I saw a few white globes float along as well. I was filled with such joy and love that I cried. There was no sadness. I had just witnessed Anna's birth into Heaven. There is such love and beauty to behold at this time in one's life and for a split second, I get to see Heaven.

When I went to Anna's home and viewed her body afterwards, she looked so relaxed and content. Everyone felt sad but at the same time they were at peace. I held each person for a while and let them cry. This love radiated from God through me to them and as they felt this love, they started to know that everything was fine. It is all so beautiful to be a part of this process of birthing someone into Heaven. Anna is home now with God. She is now, as he created her in Heaven, his Holy Child. They are together, once again, in perfect Love.

With love, Rod

THE BIG LET GO

When I was working on my master's degree in Southern California in the mid-1960s, I lived next door to Alan Hunter, an author and pacifist who had been a friend of Aldous Huxley's. Alan gave me a copy of a letter Aldous sent to several of his friends after the death of his first wife, Maria. Later, I met Laura Huxley, Aldous' second wife, when she came to speak at Girl's Collegiate School in Claremont, where I was serving as a chaplain and teacher. Laura's book, *You Are Not the Target*, had just been released and I found it fascinating reading—kind of a prelude to the Course saying, "Beware of the temptation to see yourself as being unfairly treated" (T-26.X.4:1). After that Laura and I became friends. When I wrote my first book, *Learning to Die*, in 1973, I wrote to Laura and asked her permission to reprint Aldous' letter. She wrote back saying it would be fine. Aldous described the last few minutes with Maria, how he sat by her bed and spoke to her:

> "Let go, let go, forget the body, leave it laying here like a bundle of old clothes, allow yourself to be carried as a child is carried, into the heart of the rosy light of love." She knew what love was, had been capable of love as few human beings are capable. Now she must go forward into love, must permit herself to be carried into love, deeper and deeper into it, so that at last she would be capable of loving as God loves—of loving everything, infinitely, without judging, without condemning, without either craving or abhorring. Let her forget the past, leave her old memories behind. Regrets, nostalgias, remorse, apprehensions—all these were barriers between her and the light.

The breathing became quieter and I had the sense there was some kind of release. I went on with my suggestions reducing them to their simplest form and repeating them close to her ear. "Let go, let go. Forget the body; leave it lying here; it is of no importance now. Go forward into the light. Let yourself be carried into the light. No memories, no regrets, no looking backwards, no apprehensive thoughts about your own or anyone else's future. Only this light; only this pure being, this love, this joy; above all this peace. Peace in this timeless moment, peace now, peace now." When the breathing cased, at about six, it was without any struggle.

You who are part of God are not at home except in His peace.
If peace is eternal, you are at home only in eternity.

T-5.III.10:7–8

Afterword

A mind and body cannot both exist.
Make no attempt to reconcile the two,
for one denies the other can be real.
If you are physical, your mind is gone from your self-concept,
for it has no place in which it could be really part of you.
If you are spirit,
then the body must be meaningless to your reality.

W-96.3:4–7

A mind and a body cannot both exist because a body is temporal and Mind is Eternal. While Spirit (Mind) is everlasting, all bodies disappear in time.

Reality is everything,
and you have everything because you are real.

T-9.I.13:3

Spirit need not be taught, but the ego must be.

T-4.I.3

THE WORLD IS A SCHOOL

For the ego, this world is a hiding place from God. The Holy Spirit, however, knows how to use everything as a tool for our awakening. Every mystical, spiritual, or metaphysical school of thought I know says that this world is a school and this is a "course" in miracles. As this world is a school, it is a good idea to learn what it has to teach, so that we can graduate. When we graduate, we get to go Home. Going Home means living a life with God, free of illusions and pain.

While we are not bodies, while we are here in this body, in this time, it is helpful to keep these *learning devices* working as well as we can for as long as we can, since we are here for a reason. Reality has been temporarily lost to us through the ego's usurpation. The ego has tried in vain to wrestle God's Kingdom from Him by persuading us to make up our own little kingdoms. Making up our own little world means living in a dream, a fantasy from which we must awaken. God is not angry or upset with us because we dream unhappy dreams. How could God not be God? Only the ego's god is an angry god. God forgave us before anything ever happened. That is what "for-giveness" means. For this very reason—nothing has happened. We never lost our place in the Kingdom.

Happy dreams are heralds of the dawn of truth upon the mind.
They lead from sleep to gentle waking, so that dreams are gone.
And thus they cure for all eternity.

W-140.3:3–5

We are all destined to remember Home—the sooner, the happier. Our nightmares must turn to happy dreams before the dreaming ends. Shifting from a life of struggle to one of receiving guidance involves a willingness to heal. Though we may not yet be in Heaven, though we may not yet remember what enlightenment means—it is still possible, even today, to completely let every unforgiveness go. Thus, do we begin at last to dream a happy dream. Heaven is for sure—even here, even now. It is no dream to love our brothers as ourselves (T-18V.1). Salvation is a happy dream of awakening.

Spirit is in a state of grace forever.
Our reality is only spirit.
Therefore we are in a state of grace forever.

T-1.III.5:4–6

An illusion can never replace reality. God pays no attention to our insanity, knowing it is foolishness. We need not die in order to return Home. Eternity is in the Mind. As the Course says, "Why wait for Heaven?"

The ego's lesson seems harsh only because the ego makes it that way. In the light of everlasting truth, the ego disappears back into the nothingness from which it came. Just like last night's dream, *poof*, it is gone, and we awaken from the illusion of who we thought we were in acknowledgment of the beautiful truth of our Eternal Being.

As my friend, Veronica Viddler, discovered when she had a heart attack, and as I discovered when I had cancer, what we call death is seen as Life when we trust in God and let illusion go. God is in charge and all is well. As the illusory ego disappears, Spirit steps forward and takes its place as our lasting reality. How do we get Home? Though it may look hard, the path is easy. All that is needed is the acceptance of responsibility for the life we have made, and then we make a simple choice: to see it differently, to see it the way God created it.

GOOD MORNING

What awaits each of us is so far beyond individuality and egoistic personhood that nothing is left of this old world, save for the Love that gives us Life. Spirit coming Home is always an awakening from a dream. A friend told me that her mother's last words were "Good morning!" and then I read that the last words of William

Muhlenberg, the founder of St. Luke's Hospital in New York City, were "Good morning!" To what or to whom do you think they were speaking? Were they dying or were they waking up?

We call it death, but it is liberty.
It does not come in forms that seem to be thrust down in pain
upon unwilling flesh, but as a gentle welcome to release.

If there has been true healing, this can be the form in which death
comes when it is time to rest a while
from labor gladly done and gladly ended.

Now we go in peace to freer air and gentler climate,
where it is not hard to see the gifts we gave were saved for us.

For Christ is clearer now;
His vision more sustained in us;
His Voice, the Word of God, more certainly our own.

S-3.II.3:1–5

Acknowledgments

We are all indebted to Dr. Kenneth Wapnick and his wife, Gloria, for the example they set as guides on the path Home.

My thanks to Judy Whitson of the Foundation for Inner Peace for her friendship of nearly fifty years; it was Judy who helped with the connections that made this book possible.

My assistant, Fran Cosentino, helped in every stage of development. I am grateful to her for her editorial skills, diligence, and patience.

I'm very appreciative of the help of *Course in Miracles* students/teachers: Lynne Matous, Gregg Matous, David Brown, Lorri Coburn, Ken Mallory, and Reverend Heather Harris for the many hours they spent looking over this book and making suggestions for improvements.

My friend, Shanti Rica Josephs, has since 1972 been my steady rock—the one to whom I've been able to pour out my soul, the one who has consistently known the right answer.

I am grateful for the consistent, kind guidance of my agent, Ivor Whitson; his wife, Ronnie; and my editor, Kate Zimmermann, at Sterling Publishing.

At the top of the list go my thanks to my wife, my partner in life, my darling Dolores, who is ever-present in her love and devotion to the life we share. Loving her is my greatest happiness. I am a very lucky man. The day I met Dolores was the best day of my life. She brought me my daughter, Sarah—a shining light in my life.

Index

About the Author

Jon Mundy, PhD, is an author and lecturer and the Executive Director of All Faiths Seminary International in New York City. He taught university courses in philosophy and religion from 1967 to 2009. He is the publisher of *Miracles* magazine and the author of ten books, including his bestselling book, *Living A Course in Miracles*. He is also the Senior Minister Emeritus of Interfaith Fellowship in New York City. He met Dr. Helen Schucman, the scribe of *A Course in Miracles*, in 1973. Helen introduced Jon to the Course and served as his counselor and guide until she became ill in 1980. Jon also appears on occasion as Dr. Baba Jon Mundane, a stand-up philosopher comedian.

If you enjoyed this book, you might enjoy watching regular monthly presentations by Jon on YouTube.

You might also enjoy a subscription to *Miracles* magazine.

Visit: www.miraclesmagazine.org

Box 1000, Washingtonville, NY 10992

Or call: 212-866-3795